REEL MASTERS

CHEFS CASTING ABOUT WITH TIMING & GRACE

REEL MASTERS

JEREMIAH BACON | JOHN BESH | WALTER BUNDY | JOHN CURRENCE
KELLY ENGLISH | CHRIS HASTINGS | DONALD LINK | KEVIN WILLMANN

SUSAN SCHADT

PHOTOGRAPHY BY LISA BUSER
FOREWORD BY PETER KAMINSKY
EDITED BY SUSAN SCHADT

SUSAN SCHADT PRESS

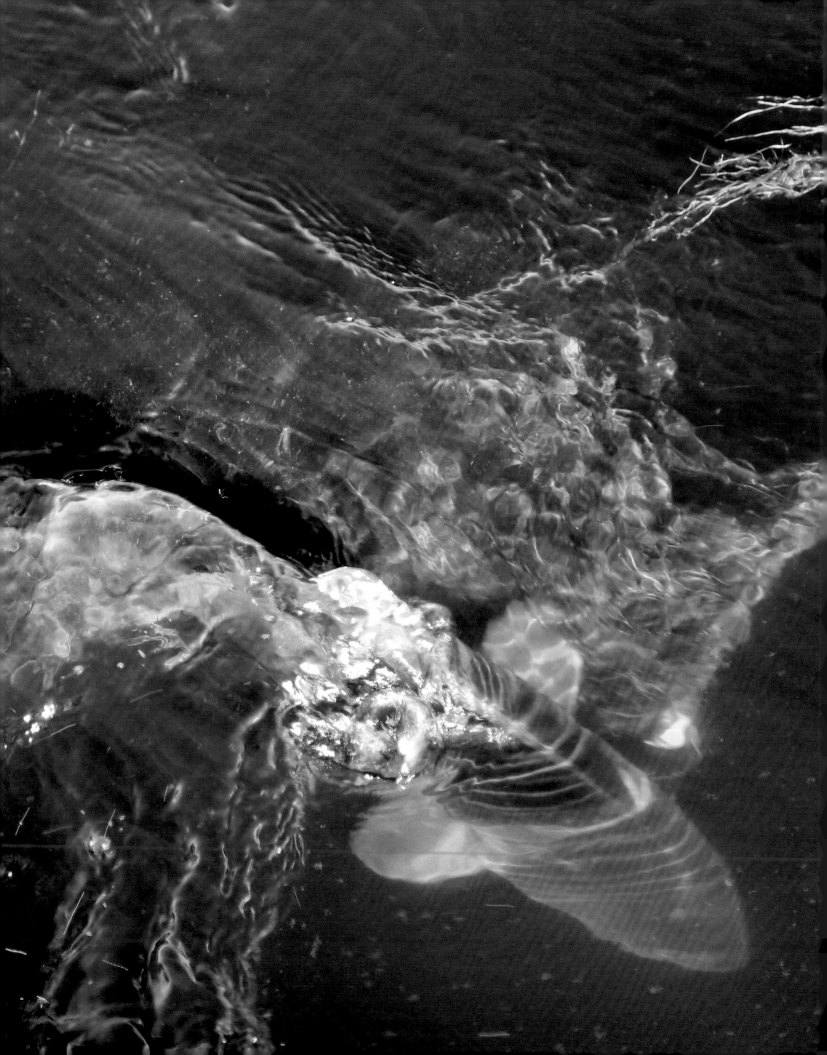

YESTERDAY, TODAY, AND NEXT TIME

There are many things that I love about fishing. One of them—maybe not even the most important one—is fish. I also treasure sunset on the water and moonrise over the hills, peanut butter and banana sandwiches wrapped in wax paper, friends I haven't seen for too long, yet, whenever we fish, it's as if no time at all has gone by. I thrill at the strong sense, just before a fish hits, that the water is somehow pregnant. I marvel at the towering thunderhead bearing down and the calculation of "how much time do I have before I have to crank up and run for shelter?" And at day's end, after the gear is put away and the fish cleaned and gutted, there's the soothing melody of ice in a rocks glass as you pour whiskey in it and the way it catches the firelight as you wait for your cooking coals to whiten over with ash.

EVERY CHEF in this book—in fact every angler I know—has fond memories like these. They always come out sounding like poetry, or phrases from a holy trance. That may be part of the allure of this ancient pastime. Fishing taps something in our deepest soul. I believe, fundamentally, that is because it arises out of one of our most basic drives: the quest for sustenance. Whenever we fish, we are taking part in a pursuit that is older than humanity itself. I'll bet that all creatures feel something akin to the angler's exhilaration: a trout closing in on a frantic minnow, an eagle with talons extended as it poises to snatch a rabbit, a lion about to leap on a luckless zebra. All creatures great and small need to eat, and fishing grants us a pleasure born of primal instinct.

When I fish, clocks and the passage of time have little meaning. It is always simply now. I could fish for an hour, a day, a week, and it all feels like one eternal moment. As far back as I can recall—back in the day when I was a burger flipper at summer camp—cooking has had the same effect on me. From the instant that I lift my knife to peel an onion to the first waft of aroma bearing the results of the alchemy of cuisine, I am in the moment. To me, this is one definition of pleasure: being present. Although the chefs in this book have a lot more clatter and clamor going on in their kitchens, each one will tell you that what led them to their career was a similar love of cooking.

Cooking and fishing are what make me who I am. The rest is just what I do so that I can cook and fish some more. But that only begins to tell the story. The fishermen in these pages can recount, with great affection and wistful longing, a dad or granddad rousing them from slumber in the cold early light of dawn and bundling them into the front seat of the family's car. While these younger versions of the heroes of this book were still half-asleep, listening to the struggle of the ignition until the car finally turned over and they headed for the lake, river, or shore. Or they can summon up the spirit of a grandmother who sat on a dock watching her bobber for the tell-tale sign of a blue gill about to take a fatal nibble. Or they can reawaken the sense of liberation that came with grabbing a cane pole and a can of worms on a morning that was surely made for hooky. So I stand corrected. More than being just about the present moment, fishing is as much about the memories it summons up and the ghosts of days and people gone by that come along for the ride whenever you pick up your tackle box. There's a lot of yesterday in fishing. And a lot of now.

In the years that I wrote for the "Big 3" outdoors magazines—Field & Stream, Sports Afield, and Outdoor Life—I traveled and fished frequently in the Southeast, which is where most of this book takes place. I got to know a part of the country that often seems as foreign to New Yorkers as the Khyber Pass. With the fervor of a born-again convert, I took to fried crappie, hushpuppies, country ham, sorghum molasses, barbecue, and grits.

Later, as a food writer, I discovered that alongside these ancestral foods, a new generation of chefs had adapted the mind-bogglingly rich variety of fresh ingredients with which the South is blessed. They created imaginative new recipes—many of them in this book—that delivered all the power of tradition with the finesse of master craftsmen.

Not coincidentally, every chef I met on assignment hunted and fished. I was even fortunate enough to fish with two of them in this book. Jeremiah Bacon took me for a morning's redfishing in the salt marshes north of Charleston and later cooked our catch at his restaurant along with some heritage breed pork that a farmer friend brought by. With John Besh, the meal was less of a home game. We were in Alaska judging a seafood contest and had gone fishing near the town of Homer. We boated a huge haul following which John and two fellow chefs cooked up a meal of white salmon, trout roe, wild strawberries, and chanterelles. It sounds fancy, but its simplicity stands as a testament to how a great chef can do more with less, especially when the fish is so fresh. Another of the chefs in this book, Donald Link, and I have never fished together, but it seems whenever I have gone to his restaurant, Cochon in New Orleans, we sip on a cold one and vow to fish next time.

Come to think of it, there's an awful lot of "next time" that animates the hope of every fisherman. ❀

When I fish, clocks and the passage of time have little meaning. It is always simply *now*. I could fish for an hour, a day, a week, and it all feels like one eternal moment.

REEL MASTERS: BEYOND A LIMIT

With their teeming culinary calendars, perhaps the most tempting tonic I could cast out to our eight celebrated chefs was, "Let's go fishing!" It's a potent phrase that stirs the soul of every fisherman, especially these chefs, passionate about conservation and resolutely hooked on the beloved sport. In short order, they readied their rigs, enlisted family, friends, and guides, and planned strategy and season, eager to selflessly share their stories of the country's most sought-after fishing spots and unknown gems.

HERE, THEN, is a firsthand and rare glimpse into their private fishing respites, rituals, and reflections. Part field guide, part cookbook, this sporting story is warm and potent, a familiar and soulful pull on the memory of that first fish, cherished recipes and a sport that provides no end of keen pleasure.

From their earliest recollections of youthful adventures and boyhood schemes to their grown-up versions of camaraderie, competition, and renewal, catching fish is the lure. Also passionate about the preservation of fishing for future generations and the requisite replenishment of nature and ecosystems, their collective voice imparts deep and lasting values way beyond a limit.

Stewards of the land and the water, these chefs work to make a difference. They support local farmers, sustainable conservation and fisheries, train rising chefs, and fight childhood illness. They are culinary entrepreneurs and philanthropic innovators that give back in a multitude of ways.

They are the real masters!

Lisa Buser's artful eye, with photographic genius and grit, captures the essence of the bounty and spirit of bayous, backwaters, and bays, as well as the celebration of culinary culture and the sporting life. Undaunted in her pursuit of magical moments, Lisa floats seamlessly from 10-hour cobia hunts atop a three-tiered roiling tower, through the perfect storm as it looms over a deadline, to assorted late-night, deliciously un-styled food shots.

This vivid combination of images and stories embody affection, anticipation, and gracious sharing of this thoroughly rewarding sport. Chances are that each of us would describe our days spent fishing with a similar voice.

Peter Kaminsky, author of our Foreword, offers that such portrayals, " ...always come out sounding like poetry, or phrases from a holy trance." That depiction enchanted me upon first reading and remains one of my favorite phrases in his evocative and powerful essay.

You, too, will read the narrative and borrow nuggets that beg for savoring and sharing. Like a purposeful cast with rod and reel, I wasn't quite sure where Peter was leading me, but I sure was excited when I got there. How fitting for his story of "yesterday, now, and next time." ⊛

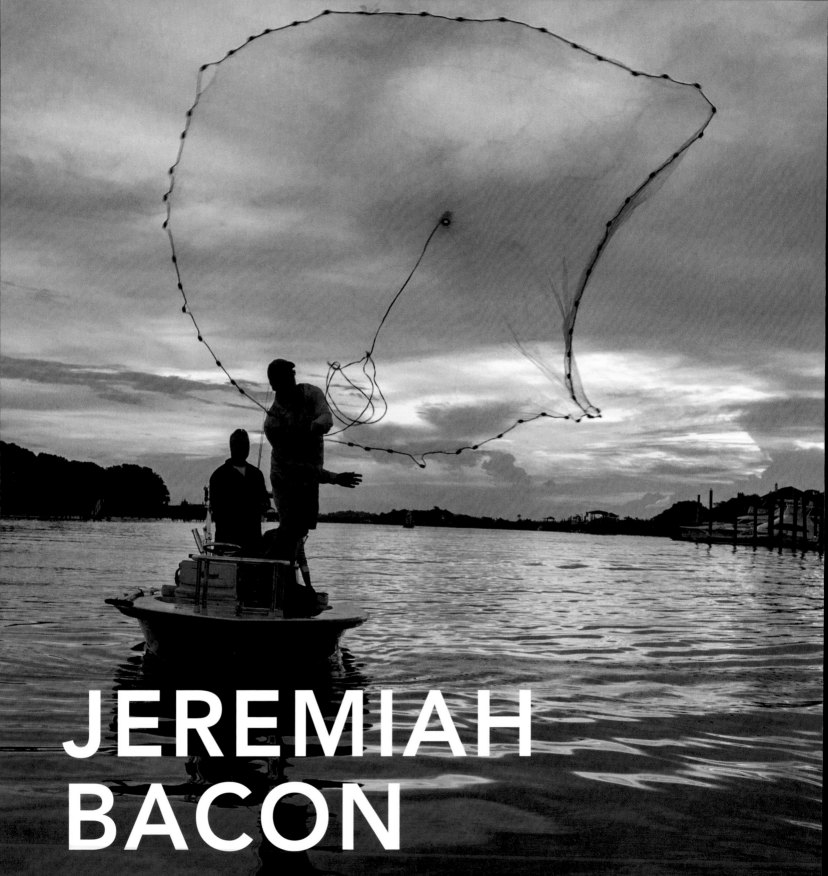

JEREMIAH
BACON

SULLIVANS
ISLAND, SC

I CAN'T BE AWAY from the water for very long. It was where I found my first sense of freedom as a teenager. I connected it to adventure, and it was just my place. It has always been where I have felt most comfortable, and it's where I return when I need to find peace and balance.

JEREMIAH BACON
CHARLESTON, SC

Bacon, a native of John's Island, S.C., is the executive chef and partner of The Oak Steakhouse and The Macintosh, which in 2012 was a semifinalist for Best New Restaurant by the James Beard Foundation, awarded best new restaurant in *Bon Appetit*'s annual 50 Best New Restaurants, and named Best New Restaurant by *Esquire*. Bacon is a five-time James Beard Foundation semifinalist for Best Chef Southeast, most recently in 2016. After culinary school at the Culinary Institute of America in Hyde Park, New York, Bacon lived in New York City, where he honed his skills in the kitchens of some of the city's most legendary restaurants, including River Café, Le Bernardin, and Per Se.

MY FIRST MEMORY of eating what I caught was with my grandmother when I was 7 or 8 years old. She would take us to a little dock on the Folly River, and we would catch blue crabs and shrimp on 3-foot lift nets. Then we would go to her house and cook them "big pot" style with corn and sausage and eat them right on her back porch with tea so sweet you could stand a spoon in it.

In the mid-80's, my family got a small jon boat with a 25-horsepower stick engine, and I was allowed to take it out by myself. It's like growing up on a farm, where kids start driving the family pickup when they are 13- or 14-years-old: you can't go too fast and there is not much to run into. It was like that with a jon boat, too, especially scooting around the barrier islands. I was a strong surfer and swimmer, and my parents felt comfortable with my friends and me heading out on our own.

We stayed pretty much on the back end of Kiawah Island and Johns Island, exploring the three rivers: Kiawah, Stone, and Folly. There was plenty of time spent in and around the creeks and throwing the cast net and fishing pole around. We would often bring back a nice cache of shrimp to the house, and watch my mom prepare and cook them — the true beginnings of my interest in learning how to cook.

There is no better way for a kid to grow up than with exposure to the outdoors, whether it's inland in the woods and fields or out on the water. It helps build awareness of the wonders of life, and it also helps build respect and regard for the dangers found in nature, especially on the open water. You have to pay attention to your surroundings and yourself. For me, those summers helped forge a lifetime of wonderment and admiration of the water.

"There is no better way for a kid to grow up than with exposure to the outdoors, whether it's inland in the woods and fields or out on the water. It helps build awareness of the wonders of life, and it also helps build respect and regard for the dangers found in nature, especially on the open water."

"Just rocking on the boat, sitting still and listening to the sound of the waves hitting the sides. It's a place that forces me to listen, watch, feel the water, and have patience. It's about what's going on in a whole other world—the one on the water and the one under it."

After graduating from the College of Charleston, I enrolled at the Culinary Institute of America, which is perched high on a cliff over the Hudson River in Hyde Park, New York. The campus was vast and beautiful. It was bitterly cold, too, especially for a kid who grew up in Charleston. I started in January and the temperature was in the 20s with a fierce wind coming off the river. I pushed myself pretty hard at school, and I would find myself looking out on the river for a few moments every day for inspiration and sometimes consolation. It was fascinating to watch such a big river push huge amounts of water and ice up and down, all day long.

I did my externship at The River Cafe, located directly beneath the Brooklyn Bridge on the East River. The restaurant was fastened to a barge, and water in the river was extremely fast-moving as it squeezed into the narrow mouth from the bay. For me, it was the perfect metaphor for the hectic pace of New York City.

I went on to work in the kitchens of Ilo, Le Bernardin, and Per Se. They were intense, high-paced environments that put out very complex dishes in a highly orchestrated setting. My winddown would involve running and the water. I began to do a lot of long distance running, and I would always plan routes near the water. I lived just a few blocks south of the George Washington Bridge, and I loved to jog across the bridge into Fort Lee, New Jersey, and down the footpath of Fort Washington Park. The immensity of the bridge and river would merge, at some points even rivaling the high energy of living in such a dynamic city.

After New York, I spent two years working in Martha's Vineyard and Boston. The coastline of the Northeast and the local seafood is so different from the Lowcountry of South Carolina, but the people who live near the water share so many qualities and have so many similar outlooks. This is even more prevalent in communities where a big part of their livelihoods are dependent on the water, whether tourism or fishing. "Water people" have a connection to each other.

Ultimately, the water helped me find my way back home. I arrived back in Charleston after 10 years, and one of the first things I did was take a boat down to Bass Creek on Kiawah. I zipped down the creek knowing where every sandbar and oyster bed was. I could do it with my eyes closed. It felt like home.

"When you buy from the folks who make their living on the land and water, you get to know their struggles and challenges, and to know the role we as customers play in that."

I landed at Carolinas Restaurant, and I knew that seafood was going to play a big part of the menu. In those days, a guy would show up at the back door with 100 pounds of mahi-mahi, already cut into filets and packed in bags of ice, the ice sitting directly on the flesh. Having grown up on the water, I knew what happens when you catch a fish, how to handle it properly to keep it pristine—and that's what I wanted to serve on my menu.

I began to seek out and meet local fisherman like Tommy Edwards (shrimper), Clammer Dave (clams and oysters), Kimberly Carroll (blue crabs), and Mark Marhefka (fisherman). At the time, few chefs—like Ben Berryhill, Nico Romo, and Charles Arena—were buying from Mark, and we used to have to go pick the fish up at the docks. A year later, Mark got a truck with a cooler on it and started delivering downtown, and that helped fuel a new outlet of local seafood by chefs all over town.

When I joined Steve Palmer at Oak Steakhouse in 2010, we introduced fresh local seafood and oysters to the classic steakhouse menu. A year later, when we opened The Macintosh, seafood played an even bigger role in what type of cuisine we serve.

Buying from local producers, whether fishermen or farmers, is very important to us. You start getting the bigger picture and the whole story by making these connections and having relationships. When you buy from the folks who make their living on the land and water, you get to know their struggles and challenges, and to know the role we as customers play in that.

We have been platinum members of the Sustainable Seafood Initiative, now known as the Good Catch Program, for the last nine years. It is a program put together by the South Carolina Aquarium that grades the seafood we are using and sourcing. We buy from local fisherman who make their living off the water, not recreational fisherman, and we take great pains to make sure they are, to use the motto of the Good Catch Program, "fishing for the future."

On down days, my wife and I get out on the water in our 15-foot creek boat. I'm extremely fortunate that she likes to fish, and she is pretty good at it, too. I get so much joy watching her catch a fish. Even if it's a stingray that jumped on her line, her excitement is peak level. Other times when the fish aren't biting we will just find a creek to tuck into and open up a bottle of wine. Those creeks are so peaceful, with long periods of silence broken only by a dolphin surfacing or an occasional plane passing overhead.

One thing that fascinates me about the water is that it seems to exist in a continuous state of duality, carrying deep, eternal themes while also speaking in a present tense. It can move forth with such a slow and heavy force and at the same time have a dynamic and wild immediacy that is full of constant life.

Out there on the water is where I feel most comfortable. Just rocking on the boat, sitting still and listening to the sound of the waves hitting the sides. It's a place that forces me to listen, watch, feel the water, and have patience. It's about what's going on in a whole other world—the one on the water and the one under it.

And, for me, it just feels like home. ✹

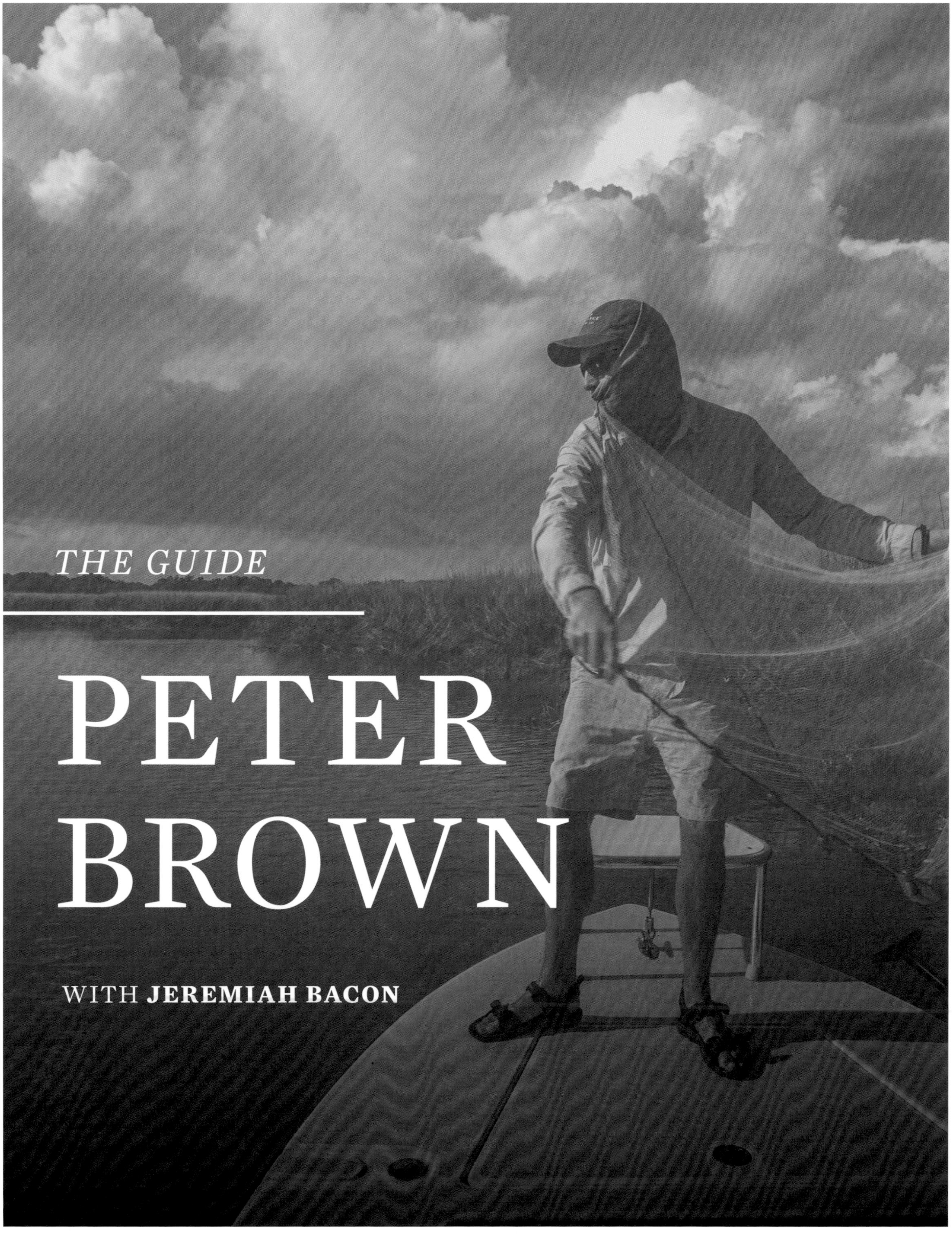

THE GUIDE

PETER
BROWN

WITH **JEREMIAH BACON**

THE LOWCOUNTRY OF SOUTH CAROLINA is home to a fishery that is considered a success story. During the 1980s, conservation initiatives banned the use of gill nets and gave several species gamefish status, meaning they could no longer be sold commercially. The fishery has rebounded. Charleston guide Peter Brown was one of the first flats guides in the area and helped pioneer shallow water sight-fishing, now a common practice. "Catching fish on a consistent basis takes an understanding of tides, weather, wind, and moon phases. Tides range from 4-8 feet, a guide has to know precisely when, where, and how to fish, often in places that would otherwise be inaccessible."

SHALLOW WATER FISHING is a more technical way of chasing fish that are wary of any loud noise or disturbance from the boat. Getting close enough to cast and hook fish is more of a stalking technique; more like hunting. It's a concerted effort between angler and guide. Communication is essential, and the guide will often spot the fish and tell the angler where to place the lure. Sometimes the right cast is just a few feet ahead of cruising fish, but often when casting to a school the approach is to cast beyond them and work the lure or fly into the fish. When people refer to fish "tailing" they are referring to high water feeding activity in which the fish are rooting for fiddler crabs in the salt marsh, often waving their tails above the surface. The cast usually needs to go within a foot or two of the fish and the main goal is just getting the fish to see the fly or lure. Sometimes the fish have to be tricked into eating the lure, but other times they devour it as soon as it hits the water.

Most schooling activity occurs during the cooler months of the year, October through March, when the water is clear, bait is less prevalent and the fish respond well to flies and artificial lures. As the water warms into spring and summer, the fish eat a variety of natural baits like blue crab, mullet, shrimp, and fiddler crabs. They will still hit lures under the right conditions and particularly love to eat a fly when they are "tailing" in the grass, which typically happens on spring tides during the new and full moons. There are other times when the tide is wind-driven and will reach heights normally only seen during those moons, thus allowing fish to access the short "hard marsh" where the fiddler crabs live. Seeing a big redfish attack a fly in a foot of water is something that people never forget.

GRILLED RED DRUM WITH SAUCE GRIBICHE

SERVES 4

Red drum is one of my favorite fish to catch and cook. This South Carolina fish is a huge conservation success story. Due to its popularity, it was becoming scarce. Fishing for it commercially was stopped for many years. Whereas it still cannot be sold commercially in South Carolina, red drum is a popular game fish here in South Carolina.

Also, I think it is the perfect fish for the home cook as it is one of the easiest fishes to get a good crispy skin. Make sure the skin of the fish is extra dry before cooking. My trick is to run the edge of a knife back and forth across the grain of the skin. It's almost like you a squeegeeing the moisture out of the skin.

Sauce Gribiche is such a great sauce for summertime and grilling. There is such a nice contrast between the chilled sauce and the hot fish. This is my version of the classic French sauce. I often call it "Broken Sauce Gribiche." Instead of emulsifying all the ingredients like in the classic version, I just toss all the ingredients in the oil. Just put all the ingredients into a container and throw it in your cooler. The sauce is ready!

FOR THE SAUCE GRIBICHE:
- 2 TEASPOONS CHOPPED CAPERS, DRAINED AND RINSED
- ½ CUP EXTRA-VIRGIN OLIVE OIL
- 2 HARD-BOILED EGGS, BOTH YOLKS AND WHITES FINELY CHOPPED
- 1 TABLESPOON FINELY CHOPPED CORNICHON PICKLES
- 1 TABLESPOON CHOPPED FRESH PARSLEY LEAVES
- 2 TEASPOONS WHOLE-GRAIN MUSTARD
- 1 TEASPOON KOSHER SALT
- 1 TABLESPOON RED WINE VINEGAR

PLACE ALL the ingredients in a medium bowl and stir to combine. Refrigerate until ready to serve.

Cooking Tip: *I recommend adding the vinegar to the Sauce Gribiche just before serving. The acid in the vinegar will turn the fresh parsley brown if left together for too long.*

FOR THE RED DRUM:
- 4 FILETS (6-OUNCE EACH) RED DRUM
- 2 TABLESPOONS OLIVE OIL
- KOSHER SALT AND FRESHLY GROUND BLACK PEPPER

PREHEAT A CLEAN grill to medium-high.

Cross hatch the skin of the fish fillets. Brush both sides of the fish with the olive oil. Season with salt and pepper to taste.

Place the fish on the grill. Close the lid and cook, turning once, until medium, about 4 to 5 minutes per side.

To serve, place the fish on the plate and top with a generous spoonful of the Sauce Gribiche.

SAMBAL CHIMICHURRI

SERVES 4 TO 6

Chimichurri is an Argentinean sauce most commonly served with red meat, but it is also delicious drizzled over grilled fish. I find it to be a really nice enhancer to any grilled dish. It gives the flavor of the char a little kiss of heat.

And I must emphasize ... a little kiss of heat. I am not a huge heat fan. I think too much heat in a sauce can detract from the dish. But if used correctly as a seasoning agent, hot sauce can really enhance a recipe. I find that ingredients like hot sauce and a squeeze of lemon juice really can help push flavors forward onto the palate.

In this recipe, I add Sambal, a spicy Southeast Asian chili sauce made from hot red chile peppers, salt, and sometimes vinegar, instead of classic hot sauce. It's a little less vinegary and acidic than some of the American hot sauces.

- 2 CUPS FRESH PARSLEY LEAVES
- ½ CUP FRESH CILANTRO LEAVES
- 1 GARLIC CLOVE, MINCED
- 1 CUP EXTRA VIRGIN OLIVE OIL
- ½ CUP WHITE WINE VINEGAR
- 3 TABLESPOONS SAMBAL CHILI SAUCE
- 3 TABLESPOONS MIRIN
- 1 TABLESPOON FRESHLY SQUEEZED LEMON JUICE
- 1 TABLESPOON FRESH OREGANO
- KOSHER SALT AND FRESHLY GROUND BLACK PEPPER

COMBINE ALL the ingredients in a food processor and pulse until the herbs and garlic are finely chopped and the sauce has come together, but not pureed. Season with salt and pepper to taste.

JO'S CRAB QUICHE

SERVES 8

This is my mom's recipe and it was the first recipe I mastered.

When I was a kid about 13 years old, we had a crab trap. I have fond memories of my grandmother taking us out to Folly Beach to catch crabs.

My grandmother was a rustic cook and would just boil up the crabs. My mother however loved to watch Julia Child and Jacques Pepin on TV. She started experimenting with their sophisticated French style of cooking. That's where she got the idea for this crab quiche.

We would pick the crabs we caught and Mom would make this recipe with the meat.

I started helping her out and discovered that cooking was fun. Plus as a growing teen, I was always hungry and this was one of my favorite dishes. So I learned to make it so I could have it whenever I wanted.

Cooking Tip: *Shrimp can be substituted for the crab meat. The shrimp should be peeled, de-veined, and cooked before adding to the quiche filling. I also recommend dicing it into small pieces.*

FOR THE PASTRY DOUGH:
- 1 ½ CUPS ALL-PURPOSE FLOUR
- ½ TEASPOON SALT
- ½ CUP COLD UNSALTED BUTTER, CUT INTO PEA-SIZE PIECES
- 1 TABLESPOON WATER

SIFT TOGETHER the flour and salt and place the mixture in a large bowl. Using a pastry blender, cut the butter into the flour mixture until crumbly. Sprinkle the water over the mixture. Blend together by gently tossing with a fork and pushing to the side of the bowl. Once the mixture is moistened and holds together, form the dough into a ball.

Flatten on a lightly floured surface and roll out the dough to 1/8-inch thickness.

Place the dough into a 9-inch pie pan, flute edges as desired. Refrigerate while making the filling.

FOR THE FILLING:
- 1 CUP SHREDDED SWISS CHEESE
- 1 CUP SHREDDED GRUYERE CHEESE
- 1 TABLESPOON ALL-PURPOSE FLOUR
- 3 LARGE EGGS
- 1 CUP LIGHT WHIPPING CREAM
- ½ TEASPOON PREPARED YELLOW MUSTARD
- ¼ TEASPOON WORCESTERSHIRE SAUCE
- ¼ TEASPOON KOSHER SALT
- DASH OF FRESHLY GROUND BLACK PEPPER
- DASH OF BOTTLED HOT PEPPER SAUCE
- 1 POUND FRESH LUMP CRAB, PICKED OF SHELLS (ABOUT 1 TO 1 ½ CUPS)

PREHEAT THE OVEN to 400°F.

In a medium bowl, toss together the cheeses with the flour. Set aside.

In another bowl, beat together the eggs, cream, mustard, Worcestershire, salt, pepper, and hot sauce.

Place 3/4 of the cheese mixture into the bottom of the prepared pie crust and spread into an even layer. Spoon the crab over the cheese in an even layer. Top with the remaining cheese mixture. Pour the egg mixture over the top.

Bake for 30 minutes, or until the egg mixture is set.

SOY PICKLED SHIITAKES

MAKES ABOUT 1 CUP

Have you had pickled mushrooms? If not, you must try them. They are delicious on their own ... but I always like to mix the pickled mushrooms with sautéed mushrooms. The two preparations together make such a great flavor contrast.

We have a wonderful abbey nearby that grows mushrooms. They are a supplier for the restaurant ... and my personal table. Two of my favorites are their shiitakes and their oyster mushrooms. Both of these have such solid flavor.

I make pickled mushrooms with the shiitakes ... and then toss them with sautéed oyster mushrooms.

The best way to sauté the mushrooms is simply. Just use butter, chicken stock, and salt and pepper. To finish them off, toss in some minced fresh herbs.

And serve this combo like I do ... spooned over fluffy Carolina Gold rice.

FOR THE ROASTED MUSHROOMS:
- 2 CUPS SHIITAKE MUSHROOMS
- 1 ½ TABLESPOONS OLIVE OIL
- KOSHER SALT

FOR THE PICKLING SAUCE:
- 2 TEASPOONS KOSHER SALT
- 2 TEASPOONS FRESHLY GROUND BLACK PEPPER
- 1 CUP SUGAR
- 2 CUPS RICE WINE VINEGAR
- 1 CUP CIDER VINEGAR
- 1 ½ CUPS SOY SAUCE
- 1 JALAPEÑO, MINCED
- 3 TABLESPOONS GROUND GINGER
- 2 TABLESPOONS MUSTARD SEEDS
- 1 TABLESPOON CORIANDER SEEDS
- 1 ½ CUPS EXTRA-VIRGIN OLIVE OIL

PREHEAT THE OVEN to 425°F.

Toss the mushrooms, olive oil, and salt to taste in a bowl. Spread on a baking sheet in an even layer. Roast, stirring a few times, until tender and browned, 30 to 35 minutes. Set aside to cool.

In a bowl, whisk together all the pickling sauce ingredients except the olive oil. Place the roasted mushrooms in a plastic container, cover with the pickling sauce, and then add the olive oil. Cover and refrigerate for up to 2 weeks
.

CAROLINA GOLD RICE

SERVES 4 TO 6

Carolina Gold is a delicate long-grain rice grown here at home in the Carolinas. There is a lot of heritage behind this rice and I am excited this locally-grown ingredient is regaining popularity. Charleston was built on rice. It is part of our history and one of the few crops we can grow here due to our warm weather and low country.

Before cooking this rice, be sure to rinse it several times. This will eliminate all the extra starch and help give you a fluffy finished product.

- 2 TABLESPOONS UNSALTED BUTTER
- 2 CUPS CAROLINA GOLD RICE
- 1 GARLIC CLOVE, MINCED
- 4 CUPS WATER
- 1 TEASPOON KOSHER SALT

PLACE THE RICE in a colander and rinse under cold water.

In a medium saucepot, melt the butter over medium-high heat. Stir in the rice and garlic and cook until translucent, about 1 minute. Slowly stir in the water. Add the salt.

Over high heat, bring the mixture to a boil. Reduce the heat to medium-low, cover, and simmer until the rice is tender and the liquid is absorbed, about 20 to 25 minutes.

Remove the lid and fluff the rice with a fork. Serve warm.

"One thing that fascinates me about the water is that it seems to exist in a continuous state of duality, carrying deep, eternal themes while also speaking in a present tense. It can move forth with such a slow and heavy force and at the same time have a dynamic and wild immediacy that is full of constant life."

JOHN
BESH

FISHERMEN: John Besh | Andrew Besh | Drew Mire
Patrick Berrigan, Jr | Patrick Berrigan, III | Jeff Rogers

BEING REARED IN SOUTHEAST LOUISIANA, with its vibrant shallow salt-marsh estuaries that breed life for the entire Gulf of Mexico ecosystem, informed my palate at a very young age. I vividly remember cane-pole fishing for bull croaker along these very bays and bayous I fish today with my children. Those experiences of long ago instilled a love and respect for our marsh and the foodways it gives birth to.

DELACROIX, LA

JOHN BESH
NEW ORLEANS, LA

Besh's restaurants include: August, a Gayot Top 40 Restaurant, Wine Enthusiast Top 100 Restaurant, and two time James Beard Award, Outstanding Restaurant nominee, Besh Steak, Lüke, Lüke San Antonio, La Provence, Domenica, Pizza Domenica, Borgne, Johnny Sánchez New Orleans and Baltimore, Shaya, and Willa Jean. Eunice, in Houston, is scheduled to open late 2017. Food & Wine's Top 10 Best New Chefs in America and the James Beard Foundation Award for Best Chef Southeast in 2006. Four cookbooks: *My New Orleans* (2009), *My Family Table* (2011), *Cooking from the Heart* (2013), and *Besh Big Easy* (2015, all Andrews McMeel Publishing). Hosted two national public television shows based on his books.

I WAS BLESSED with an avid outdoorsman as a father, and I found my identity as a boy by losing myself deep in the briny hot marsh in the spring and summer. As children we tried it all. We were fly fishing for reds with popping bugs, casting double sparkle beetles for specks, trawling with our 16-foot net for brown shrimp, thrashing scoop nets in the grassy shallows for soft shells, crabbing with chicken necks and hoop nets, running trot lines, gigging for flounder, casting dead shrimp at crab trap floats hoping for a blackfish to bite, and frogging with flashlights in the starlit night.

The marsh has a sound of its own, from the humming of bugs' wings to the faint drumming of the diesel oyster luggers and shrimp boats, the splashing of lake runners and reds feeding on the brackish surface while nutria call out. I found them all captivating and peaceful.

We ate what the marsh gave us, cooked based on what our delicious culture passed on. When I came home with a meaty redfish, it would be stewed down with onions, garlic, celery, Creole tomatoes, crabmeat, and shrimp into a luscious court bouillon and served over rice. If I came home with specked trout, the flaky white filets would be dredged into flour and sautéed with brown butter, lemon juice, and parsley for a heck of a trout meuniere or almandine, if mom had some almonds to add to the pan. The croakers we'd pan-fry whole and pick its sweet flesh from the bone.

The combination of our rich ecology and deep cultural traditions has allowed me effortlessly to represent our region as a chef and steward of these great traditions. I consider it an honor to be in a position today to use our many resources to help sustain these crucial but fragile wetlands through a variety of programs.

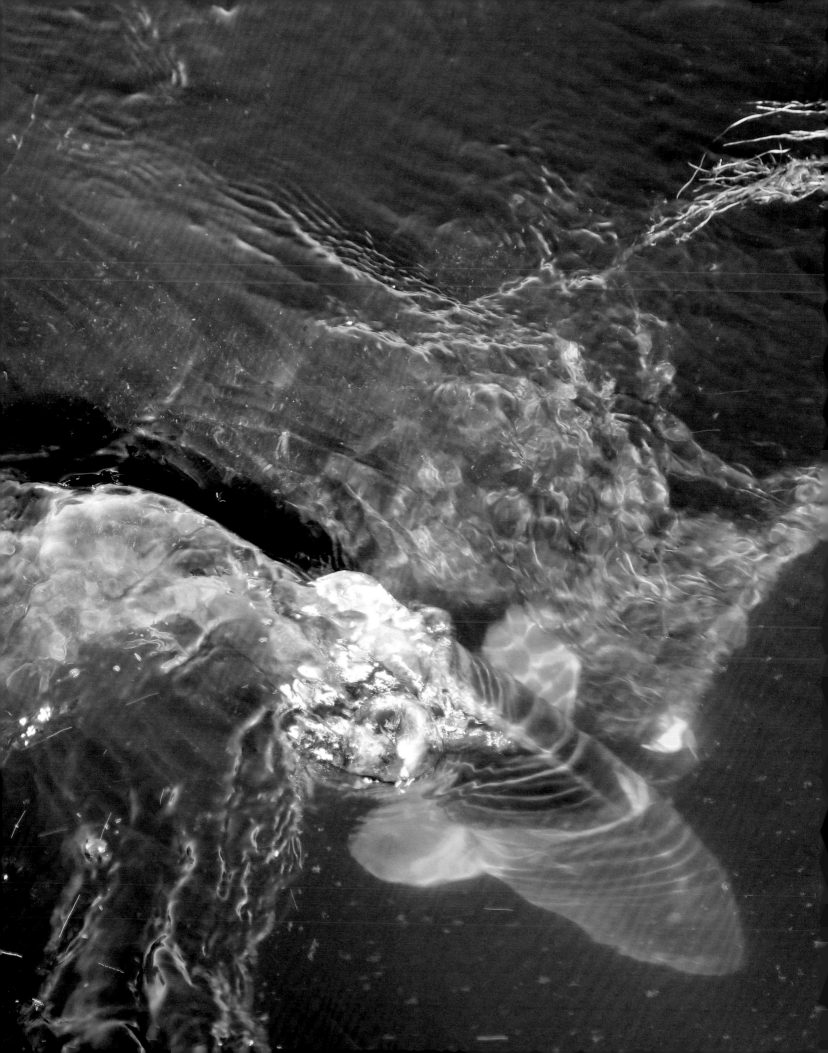

One could easily say that I have not evolved much since those early days of my idyllic youth. I am just as comfortable today lost in the Louisiana marsh with those same fellows I once fished with as a child as I am in one of our kitchens. I am blessed to be living on the same bayou that I started on, surrounded by the same fellows that I've hunted and fished with in these very marshes my entire life. I now have the honor of passing this beautiful tradition along to my sons, allowing them to grow in their affection and understanding of this bountiful and complex landscape as I did many decades ago.

Today I have the opportunity to take my youngest son Andrew, or Drew Drew, on a fishing trip with my lifelong friends: Jeff Rogers, Drew Mire, my business partner, Patrick Berrigan, my brother-in-law, and his son, Big Pat. We are hunting for red drum (or reds) deep into the shallow ponds of the Delacroix marsh. Fishing from Jeff's tower boat, designed with an extremely shallow draft and an 8-foot tower, allows us to spot the reds and cast artificial lures out in front of the fish and reel the bait just over them, creating a scenario that the fish often finds too tempting to resist.

Jeff, acting as our guide and teacher, is targeting redfish with certain genetic traits that distinguish these redfish from those most often found off-shore. These are only found in the shallow clear waters of Delacroix, where they develop a deep bronze color and are shorter, stockier, and have more girth than the reds in other areas.

Targeting fish is a bit more challenging but much more exciting. The water clarity is crucial when spotting the fish, so it's best to target fish on a sunny day with falling high tide.

"The reds race to the buoyant lure, break the surface with a sequence of mighty splashes. Hooking our first fish is dramatic, especially as our lighter tackle makes for a heck of a fight, which I gladly pass on to Drew Drew."

Wearing polarized sunglasses and dark-brimmed caps, we can see fish in the shallow waters finning their way through the grass beds, feeding on baitfish, small crabs, and brown shrimp. Drew Drew and I cast more often than not right on top of our targeted fish, spooking them and forcing us to find more targets. Eventually we get the hang of leading the fish by a couple of yards with our casts as Jeff or Drew poles the boat in the foot-deep water.

The reds race to the buoyant lure, break the surface with a sequence of mighty splashes. Hooking our first fish is dramatic, especially as our lighter tackle makes for a heck of a fight, which I gladly pass on to Drew Drew.

His face lights up with excitement and a sweet impish grin as we continue to pass him the rods to reel in the ferociously fighting reds. I jump to net them as he works them close to the boat. It's safe to say every man on the boat reverted back to the 11-year-old version of himself, giggling, laughing, and bragging about who has landed the biggest one or who could cook the best fish.

Realizing that Drew Drew will inherit the very love of the marsh from my friends and me that I took from my dear father and his friends fills my soul with happiness. Through that love of our rich ecosystem, the truest sense of stewardship evolves. Knowing that our children have that same attachment brings me deep pride as I watch the next generation of conservationists being formed through an exceptional morning of fishing in the salt marsh. ⊛

"Realizing that Drew Drew will inherit the very love of the marsh from my friends and me that I took from my dear father and his friends fills my soul with happiness."

"One could easily say that I have not evolved much since those early days of my idyllic youth. I am just as comfortable today lost in the Louisiana marsh with those same fellows I once fished with as a child as I am in one of our kitchens."

"The marsh has a sound of its own, from the humming of bugs' wings to the faint drumming of the diesel oyster luggers and shrimp boats, the splashing of lake runners and reds feeding and on the brackish surface while nutria call out. I found them all captivating and peaceful."

CREOLE SEAFOOD JAMBALAYA

SERVES 6

In Cajun country, they wouldn't think of using tomato in their Jambalaya. In New Orleans, we do like our tomato, but not too much. We don't want it looking like Spanish Rice. What's really important is to not overcook the shrimp. You want them gorgeous and plump. I add them at the very end and try not to stir the pot too often to check on them.

- ½ POUND ANDOUILLE OR OTHER SMOKED SAUSAGE, CHOPPED
- 1 POUND FRESH PORK SAUSAGE, REMOVED FROM THE CASINGS
- ½ CUP BACON FAT OR CANOLA OIL
- 1 LARGE ONION, CHOPPED
- 1 BELL PEPPER, SEEDED AND CHOPPED
- 1 STALK CELERY, WITH LEAVES, CHOPPED
- 3 GARLIC CLOVES, MINCED
- 2 CUPS WHITE RICE
- 1 TEASPOON DRIED THYME
- 2 BAY LEAVES
- 1 TEASPOON CAYENNE PEPPER
- 1 CUP CRUSHED TOMATOES
- 4 CUPS CHICKEN STOCK
- 1 ½ POUNDS MEDIUM WILD AMERICAN SHRIMP, PEELED AND DEVEINED
- KOSHER SALT AND FRESHLY GROUND BLACK PEPPER
- 2 GREEN ONIONS, CHOPPED

HEAT A VERY big heavy-bottomed pot over high heat, then reduce the heat to medium. This lets the pot heat uniformly, preventing hot spots which are likely to burn. Brown the Andouille and pork sausage in the bacon fat, stirring slowly with a long wooden spoon to build color.

After the sausages have browned, add the onions and let them caramelize for about 15 minutes to build more flavor. I add the bell peppers late, to save as much of the color as I can. Add the celery (I always use the leaves, too) and garlic, and cook for about 5 minutes, stirring occasionally so that everything cooks evenly.

Next add the rice, thyme, bay leaves, and cayenne to the pot and cook, stirring often, for about 3 minutes. Increase the heat to high, add the tomatoes and stock. Bring the liquid to a boil, then reduce the heat to medium-low, cover, and simmer for 15 minutes.

While the rice is cooking, season the shrimp with salt and pepper. After the rice has simmered for 15 minutes, fold in the shrimp and green onions. Cover again, turn off the heat and let everything continue to cook in the pot for another 10 minutes. Remove the lid, fluff the jambalaya, and serve!

Recipe from *Besh Big Easy*
(Andrews McMeel Publishing, 2015)
Photograph © Maura McEvoy

STUFFED ARTICHOKES

SERVES 6

In New Orleans, we make Stuffed Artichokes as an offering of abundance at St. Joseph's Day feasts. They're sold stuffed and ready-to-go at many little food shops around town. We consider them "social food:" a dish you'd put in the middle of the table. Just one look at these abundant artichokes and you know: "This is something good!"

- 3 LARGE OR 6 SMALL ARTICHOKES
- 3 GARLIC CLOVES, THINLY SLICED
- 1 ¼ CUPS OLIVE OIL, DIVIDED
- 1 TEASPOON CRUSHED RED PEPPER FLAKES
- 2 CUPS DRIED BREADCRUMBS
- 1 CUP GRATED PARMESAN CHEESE
- 1 SPRIG BASIL, CHOPPED
- 1 POUND MEDIUM WILD AMERICAN SHRIMP, PEELED, DEVEINED, AND CHOPPED
- KOSHER SALT AND FRESHLY GROUND BLACK PEPPER
- 1 POUND CRABMEAT, PICKED OF SHELLS
- 2 GREEN ONIONS, CHOPPED
- PINCH OF HERBES DE PROVENCE

PREHEAT OVEN TO 350°F.

Cut the stems off the artichokes, peel away the bottom leaves, and trim the spines off the leaves. Simmer the artichokes in a big pot of salted water for about 20 minutes. Remove and drain upside down on paper towels.

Make the stuffing by sweating the garlic in 1 cup of the olive oil in a large skillet over medium heat. Add the pepper flakes and breadcrumbs, cook 3 minutes to toast the crumbs, then remove from the heat and fold in the Parmesan and basil.

Season the shrimp with salt and pepper and sauté in 2 tablespoons of the olive oil for 2 minutes, then add the crabmeat, green onions, and Herbes de Provence. Add the stuffing mixture and stir to combine. Spoon the stuffing in between the leaves of the artichoke, the more the better!

Once the artichokes are stuffed, drizzle the remaining oil over the tops. Place the artichokes in a baking dish and cover with aluminum foil. Bake for 35 minutes. Then remove the foil and bake for an additional 10 to 15 minutes, or until the stuffing is golden brown.

Recipe from *Besh Big Easy*
(Andrews McMeel Publishing, 2015)
Photograph © Maura McEvoy

MAMMA'S SEAFOOD GUMBO

SERVES 10

When I say I cook at home more and more like my mother and grandmother did, this gumbo is a great example. Cooking it makes me so happy! I get that deep shellfish flavor from cooking the crabs at least 45 minutes before adding the other seafood. It's all about tasting, adjusting the flavors, and really just cooking from your heart.

- ¾ CUP CANOLA OIL
- ¾ CUP ALL-PURPOSE FLOUR
- 2 LARGE ONIONS, CHOPPED
- 6 BLUE CRABS, QUARTERED
- 1 STALK CELERY, CHOPPED
- 4 GARLIC CLOVES, MINCED
- 3 QUARTS SHRIMP OR SHELLFISH STOCK
- 2 CUPS SLICED OKRA
- 1 TABLESPOON FRESH OR DRIED THYME
- 2 BAY LEAVES
- 1 POUND SMOKED SAUSAGE, SLICED ½-INCH THICK
- 4 GREEN ONIONS, CHOPPED
- 2 TABLESPOONS CREOLE SPICE
- KOSHER SALT AND FRESHLY GROUND BLACK PEPPER
- TABASCO®
- 1 POUND MEDIUM WILD AMERICAN SHRIMP, PEELED AND DEVEINED
- 1 CUP SHUCKED OYSTERS AND THEIR LIQUOR
- 1 CUP CRABMEAT, PICKED OF SHELLS
- 6 CUPS WARM WHITE RICE, COOKED AS PER PACKAGE INSTRUCTIONS

MAKE A ROUX by heating the oil in a large heavy-bottomed pot over high heat. Whisk the flour into the hot oil. It will immediately begin to sizzle. Reduce the heat to medium and continue whisking until the roux turns a deep brown color, about 15 minutes. Add the onions, stirring them into the roux with a wooden spoon. Lower the heat to medium low and continue stirring until the roux turns a glossy dark brown, about 10 minutes.

Add the blue crabs and stir for a minute to toast the shells, then add the celery and garlic. Raise the heat to medium and cook, stirring, for 3 minutes. Add the stock, okra, thyme, and bay leaves. Bring the gumbo to a boil, stirring occasionally. Reduce the heat to medium low and simmer for 45 minutes. Stir occasionally and skim off the fat from the surface of the gumbo (moving the pot half off the burner helps collect the impurities).

Add the sausage and green onions to the pot and cook for 15 minutes. Season well with the Creole spice, salt, pepper, and Tabasco®. Add the shrimp, oysters and their liquor, and crabmeat to the pot and cook for about 5 minutes. Serve over rice.

Recipe from *Besh Big Easy*
(Andrews McMeel Publishing, 2015)
Photograph © Maura McEvoy

PICKLED SHRIMP

SERVES 10

This recipe requires high-quality wild shrimp. Of course, I prefer wild Louisiana shrimp from the water I know. It's better to find the best shrimp than to worry about whether they've been frozen or not. Unless the shrimp come straight from the net to your kitchen, sometimes the highest quality options are frozen. This is where a trusty fishmonger makes all the difference.

You can mix up your vegetables with the shrimp, using whatever's fresh and local. I love to add cauliflower, carrots, daikon, beans, onions, militon, and/or okra.

FOR THE BRINE:

- 2 CUPS RICE WINE VINEGAR
- ZEST AND JUICE OF 1 LEMON
- ZEST AND JUICE OF 1 ORANGE
- ½ CUP SUGAR
- 5 GARLIC CLOVES, THINLY SLICED
- 1 TABLESPOON CORIANDER SEEDS
- 1 TABLESPOON MUSTARD SEEDS
- 1 TABLESPOON PEPPERCORNS
- 1 TABLESPOON RED CHILI FLAKES
- 2 BAY LEAVES
- PINCH OF KOSHER SALT

COMBINE all the ingredients in a large saucepan. Add 2 1/2 cups water and bring to a boil. Remove from the heat and allow to cool slightly.

FOR THE SHRIMP:

- 12 BABY CARROTS
- 12 BABY BEANS
- 12 PEARL ONIONS, PEELED
- 12 OKRA PODS
- 2 POUNDS BOILED WILD AMERICAN SHRIMP, PEELED AND DEVEINED

PACK ALL THE the vegetables and shrimp into a very large glass jar, alternating layers. Pour the hot brine into the jar to cover. Cover the jar and let cool. Refrigerate overnight. Serve right from the jar when you're ready.

Recipe from *My Family Table*
(Andrews McMeel Publishing, 2011)
Photograph © Maura McEvoy

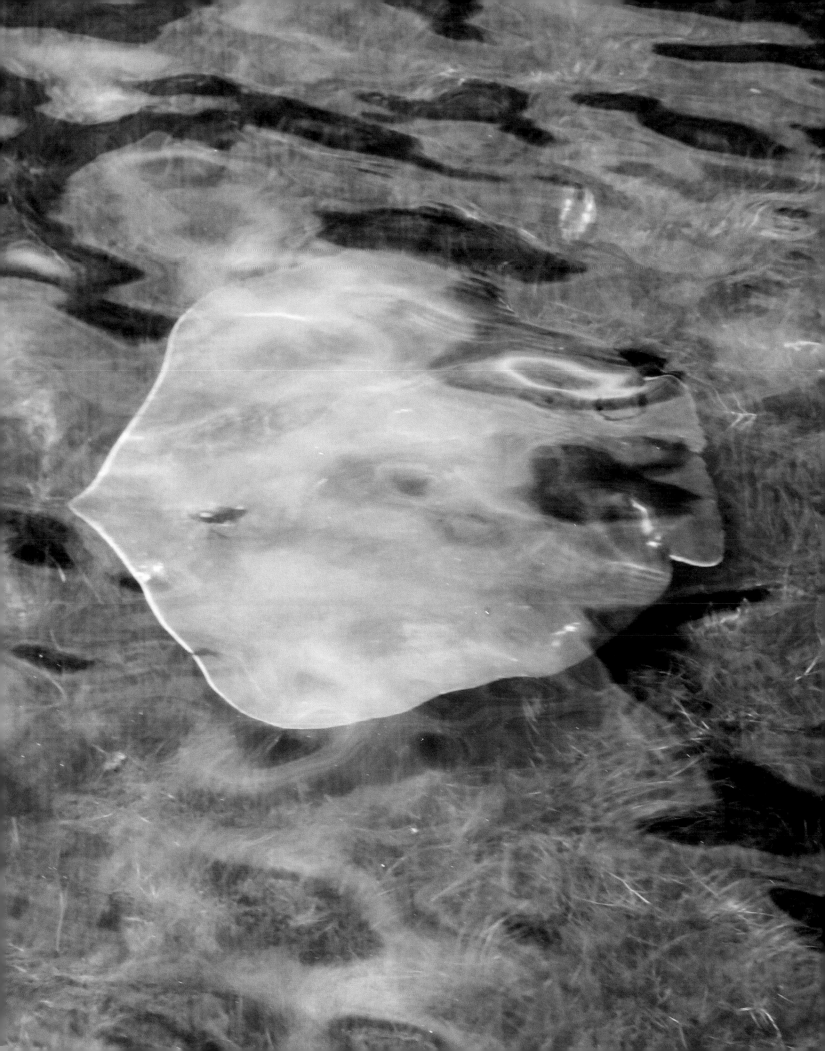

WALTER BUNDY

FISHERMEN: Walter Bundy | Bruce Edwards
Tom Gallivan | Todd Janeski

CHESAPEAKE
BAY, VA

MAN VERSUS FISH: it all comes down to that. It's that indescribable feeling of having a fishing rod in your hand and a fish pulling on the other end. It's that indescribable joy of reeling a fish in. At its most basic, it's about that innate desire and predisposition to catch food, which has been in our DNA since the beginning of time.

WALTER BUNDY
RICHMOND, VA

Bundy is executive chef and owner of Shagbark, opened July 2016, with a goal to showcase the enormous bounty of Virginia by becoming a stage for local farmers, fishermen, and artisans. He cooked in the kitchens of Thomas Keller's The French Laundry in Napa Valley and Mark Miller's Coyote Café in Santa Fe and appeared at the James Beard House, on Food Network's *Food Nation with Bobby Flay* and Cooking Channel's *Road Trip with G. Garvin*. Spent two decades at the highly acclaimed Lemaire Restaurant in Richmond's historic Jefferson Hotel and was Executive Chef for nearly 15 of those years.

MY EARLIEST MEMORIES of fishing are as a boy with my grandmothers—Jane Bundy and Helen Hoppe, whom we fondly called Gaga. Both of them had homes on a peninsula named Horse Point. It is near the mouth of the Piankatank River, one of the many tributaries of the Chesapeake Bay. It was on this river that I learned, as a young boy, how to fish and crab. I was at the river often and always looked forward to getting up early and walking out on the dock, eager to begin the day. Most mornings, I'd have a line in the water just as the sun was coming up, waiting for that addictive and beloved tap, tap, tap.

Gaga would tell me to carry the rods, bait, and tackle down that long set of stairs to the bottom of the steep embankment to her dock. I would set up her chair for her and then I could start fishing!

When she arrived, she was fully prepared. Gaga was funny. She always seemed to have her cigarette holder with a Benson and Hedges cigarette in it and her trusted red tumbler glass, which was usually filled with bourbon and ice in the afternoons. She would always have me bait her hook (we would use bloodworms) because she didn't want to get her hands dirty. That was what grandkids were for! She also had a mini two-foot rod that looked like a kids toy rod but was actually a very high quality rod and reel. Because of its size, it seemed to me that she could feel the bites better, or at least that's what I told myself when she out-fished me. She also had a "secret spot" off the left side of the pier that she claimed as her own personal flounder hole. Most of the time we fished for spot and croaker but occasionally we would catch a speckled trout or bluefish. She always insisted that I throw my line out with a bottom rig, get rid of the slack in the line, and "wait for the bites." I wouldn't let it sit long enough and always reel it in too fast. Sometimes the best lessons learned in life are through our mistakes.

My other grandmother, Jane, was a great cook and loved to eat crabs. She was the person who introduced me to my love of the blue crab. She taught me how to catch them with a piece of chicken at the end of some twine or fishing line. I learned how to recognize when the crabs were eating the chicken by how taut the line became and I would pull the line in ever so slowly and at the last second, come in very quickly from underneath with my dip net. I would catch a five-gallon bucket of crabs in no time and steam them with Jane in the kitchen. The smell of Old Bay, vinegar, and crabs drifting out of the kitchen in the middle of the day will never leave me. It is part of who I am. The only thing better would be eating that sweet, warm, just-cracked jumbo lump piece of crabmeat from that back leg. It just doesn't get any better.

Jane also loved to fish. Her favorite fish was striped bass, also known around this area as rockfish or stripers. Jane would always be the one to lead the charge to go out in the old 18-foot Boston Whaler to catch some big rockfish. She had a favorite fishing hole that was 60-feet deep in the middle of a river that averages about 20-25 feet in depth. We would find it by lining up our boat with a house, a channel marker, and a gap in the trees way out on Stove Point (old-school triangulating). We would use jigs that my dad, a doctor, made out of rubber surgical tubing that resembled eels. These custom rigs had an egg sinker in the front of the tube that looked like a head, two hooks coming out of the middle, and the end was spliced so it looked like a tail. Fishing was a family affair.

That's where it all started.

"Most mornings, I'd have a line in the water just as the sun was coming up, waiting for that addictive and beloved tap, tap, tap."

To me, fishing is about being out in the majestic outdoors, in God's beauty. That's my church—the ocean, the bay, and the rivers. It's a beauty I cannot describe. I am at complete peace on the water. It is a special place and feeling for me. It's like what I would imagine heaven to be.

It's also about the excitement. It's checking the chicken at the end of the string for crabs and the excitement of the unexpected and unknown that gets me fired up. It's like having a lottery ticket, because there is always a chance to win, especially with the bounty of the Chesapeake Bay: rockfish, speckled trout, spot, croaker, bluefish, drum, blue crabs, and cobia. It's a personal connection, one-on-one: how to present your bait, how deep, how much action, what weight line, what lure, etc. It's also about the conditions and learning when to go, where to go on certain winds, determining how certain spots react to different tides, temperatures, and seas. Every day is different and has its own characteristics. There's always something to learn. It's the thrill of the chase, the suspense of it, and never knowing how it's going to turn out.

There's also the camaraderie, whether it's with my sons or friends. It's a time to relax, settle in, enjoy the serenity, and talk about things that matter. It's about heightened senses: the smell of the bay, the sharpness of the sun, the sound of the waves, the humming of the motor, the birds fussing over bait, or seeing a fog bank and not knowing what's beyond that hazy screen.

One of the greatest things fishing does for me is to reinforce one of my core values in life—persistence. It's the same in cooking, hunting, and fishing. If you persist, work on doing the right thing, and never give up, it always pays off in the end.

A prime example is when I was cobia fishing with a friend, his son, and my sons, Quinn and Foster. My friend kept saying that he always catches the biggest fish at the very last moment. I told him that's not my experience, because whether it's hunting or fishing, it usually doesn't work out that way for me.

He kept nudging me to call it a day and I say, "Tide's still going out so let's just hang out a little longer." Other boats had left the sand bar at Windmill Point and conditions were just right. But there's nothing, absolutely nothing for another 30 minutes. Finally, I agree to go. But my son asks me to let him have one minute and 30 seconds more. The time passes quickly, it's time to go and he wants an additional one minute and 45 seconds. Literally, after one minute and 40 seconds, I see the tip of the rod go tap, tap, tap...wait, and wait, and then...the reel starts screaming and away she goes. After a long fight with a monster cobia, it hits the deck...high fives abound...no better feeling in the world!

"It's a personal connection, one-on-one: how to present your bait, how deep, how much action, what weight line, what lure, etc. It's also about the conditions and learning when to go, where to go on certain winds, determining how certain spots react to different tides, temperatures, and seas."

Every time I go out, I can go somewhere new. When there are calm seas, I can head east and get to Nassawaddox Creek on the Eastern Shore in 30 minutes, south, I can be at the Bay Bridge Tunnel in an hour, and northeast, Tangier Island in 45 minutes. I am blessed to live in the beautiful state of Virginia. I take nothing for granted.

That's why at our new restaurant, Shagbark, Virginia artisans blew glass lights, local craftsmen made the floor from reclaimed oak, and a potter spun artisan stoneware. Of course we work with local farmers and fishermen who take so much pride in their work. I am so fortunate to know all of these amazing people.

My wife's family farm, Weyanoke, is on the James River in Charles City County. There are some massive, very old shagbark hickory trees that grow there. Union troops came through Weyanoke over 150 years ago and burned everything to the ground. These trees were planted shortly thereafter. A storm took one down a couple of years ago and part of that tree was made into a community table for the restaurant. Shagbark will bring the community together around that table, a table with a history and an enormous amount of beauty.

There is also a massive rockfish displayed in the bar. It's 49 inches long, 29 inches in girth, and weighs 40 pounds. Catching it is one of the highlights of my fishing career, my biggest rockfish to date. I caught it on my own, on my boat without a fishing guide and with one of my best friends. We were just chasing birds and I was running a chartreuse-and-blue Stretch 25 lure way, way out back. For me, it was everything I enjoy about fishing. It was about going out at the right time, on the right tide, using the right lure, and most importantly, being at the right place. I figured it out on my own. I figured out the process and I was able to get the fish into the boat after a long and stressful fight. It was such a more exhilarating and rewarding triumph having done it on my own.

That rockfish in the bar is my nod to Chesapeake Bay fishing and represents everything that I love about fishing here in Virginia. To me, everything makes it special: the boat, the rods, the tackle, the bay, the conditions, the challenge, the lessons, the serenity, the camaraderie, the beauty, the reward, and the freedom.

Fish on! ✥

"To me, everything makes it special: the boat, the rods, the tackle, the bay, the conditions, the challenge, the lessons, the serenity, the camaraderie, the beauty, the reward, and the freedom. Fish on!"

"The smell of Old Bay, vinegar, and crabs drifting out of the kitchen in the middle of the day will never leave me. It is part of who I am. The only thing better would be eating that sweet, warm, just-cracked jumbo lump piece of crabmeat from that back leg. It just doesn't get any better."

"One of the greatest things fishing does for me is to reinforce one of my core values in life—persistence. It's the same in cooking, hunting, and fishing. If you persist, work on doing the right thing, and never give up, it always pays off in the end."

ROASTED "CLAMS VIRGINIA"

SERVES 4 TO 6

This dish is all about using the best locally-grown ingredients available in Virginia.

Some of the best stuff is right there in your backyard. There is so much cool stuff available locally here in Richmond ... and much of it could compete on a national level.

Let's start with the clams. Harvested off the Virginian Eastern Shore, Chincoteague clams are one of the most local products I can get. Raised on the sea side, these clams are super salty. When making the dish in your home, the key is to find the freshest regional clams you can get your hands on.

For the base of the Béchamel, I use a semi-soft cheese from Meadow Creek Dairy in the Virginia Highlands. Pungent and aromatic, their Grayson cheese offers a real depth of flavor and richness to this dish. Another local product I use is the Surry smoked sausage from Edwards Virginia Smokehouse. This local sausage adds a nice smoky flavor to the clams.

FOR THE GRAYSON CHEESE BÉCHAMEL:

- 2 CUPS WHOLE MILK
- 2 TABLESPOONS UNSALTED BUTTER
- ½ SWEET VIDALIA ONION, FINELY DICED
- 3 ½ TABLESPOONS ALL-PURPOSE FLOUR
- 1 FRESH BAY LEAF
- PINCH NUTMEG
- 4 OUNCES MEADOW CREEK DAIRY'S GRAYSON CHEESE (A GOOD SUBSTITUTE WOULD BE TALEGGIO OR ANY OTHER SEMISOFT, WASHED-RIND, SMEAR-RIPENED COW'S MILK CHEESE FROM A LOCAL DAIRY)

BRING THE MILK to a simmer in a medium pot and keep warm. Do not boil.

Melt the butter over medium-low heat in a small saucepan. Add the onions and sauté until translucent. Sprinkle the flour evenly over the onions and stir until coated. Cook for about 2 minutes, or until the mixture (a roux) has developed a slightly nutty aroma.

Stir the warm milk into the roux.

Add the bay leaf and a pinch of nutmeg. Bring the mixture to a simmer and let cook at a gentle simmer for 20 to 30 minutes, stirring every 4 to 5 minutes so the sauce doesn't burn the bottom of the pan.

Remove from the heat and let cool for 5 to 10 minutes. Gently whisk in the cheese until melted.

FOR THE SPINACH:

- 2 TABLESPOONS UNSALTED BUTTER
- 2 TABLESPOONS MINCED SHALLOTS
- 1 BAG (6-OUNCE) BABY SPINACH
- KOSHER SALT AND FRESHLY GROUND PEPPER

MELT THE BUTTER in a sauté pan over medium heat and add the shallots. Cook until translucent and soft. Add the spinach and season with salt and pepper. Cook until just wilted. Transfer the spinach to a colander and gently press to drain the excess liquid from the spinach. Reserve.

FOR THE CLAMS:

- 25 CHINCOTEAGUE CLAMS (OR ANY VIRGINIAN EASTERN SHORE MIDDLE NECK CLAMS THAT YOU PREFER)
- ½ CUP DICED SURRY SMOKED SAUSAGE (A NICE TASSO HAM WOULD WORK NICELY TOO), LIGHTLY BROWNED
- ½ CUP FINELY CHOPPED PEPPADEW PEPPERS
- ¼ CUP FRESHLY GRATED PARMESAN CHEESE

SHUCK OPEN THE CLAMS. Separate the two shells, throw away the top shell, and free the clam from the bottom shell (by cutting the abductor muscle). Place the clams in a container with the clam "liquor" (any juices from the clams). Reserve the bottom shells for the assembly.

TO FINISH THE DISH:
PREHEAT THE OVEN to 400°F.

Place the clamshells on a baking sheet
in an even layer. Spoon a little bit of
spinach into each clamshell, then
lay the clam on top of the spinach.
Drizzle just a little of the reserved clam
liquor over the clam and spinach.

Reheat the Grayson Cheese Béchamel
gently over low heat and spoon enough
to generously coat the entire face of
each clamshell over each clam.

Sprinkle some of the diced sausage
over the top, followed by the Peppadew
peppers, and a pinch of Parmesan cheese.

Bake until heated throughout, about
8 minutes. Then, turn the broiler on
and cook for another minute or so
until nice and golden on top, being
careful not to burn the topping.

CHESAPEAKE BAY OYSTER STEW WITH MASCARPONE GRITS, FOREST MUSHROOMS, AND BLACK PEPPER DEMI-GLACE

SERVES 4 TO 6

The grits I use in this dish when I make it at home are from Byrd Mills in Ashland, Virginia. The folks at Byrd Mills grind their grits along the bank of the South Anna River as has been done for centuries. They are a true ground corn with the chaff blown away and the cornmeal sifted out ... what remains is a thick, coarse grit. I cook these "grits" in milk with a bay leaf, and then finish them with mascarpone cheese (a sweet Italian cream cheese) to make them extra creamy and rich.

The forest mushrooms in this dish will vary according to seasonal availability. Most likely, the varieties will consist of shiitake, oyster, black trumpet, and golden chanterelle mushrooms.

And of important note ... the "stew" portion of this recipe should not be made until you are ready to serve your guests.

Cooking Tip: *I recommend cooking the bacon in advance and allowing it to drain before adding to the stew. This let's you have the smokiness of the bacon without the grease.*

FOR THE GRITS:
- ½ CUP BYRD MILLS STONE-GROUND GRITS
- 1 ½ CUPS WHOLE MILK
- 1 FRESH BAY LEAF
- 3 TABLESPOONS PLUGRÁ® UNSALTED BUTTER
- KOSHER SALT AND GROUND WHITE PEPPER
- 2 TABLESPOONS MASCARPONE CHEESE

PLACE THE GRITS, milk, and bay leaf in a 2-quart saucepot and warm over low heat. The grits should cook at just below a simmer (about 200°F) for 4 hours. These are not your everyday instant grits and therefore need frequent stirring and attention to have them evenly cooked. If they become dry and are not cooked to a fully soft stage, feel free to add more milk and cook further. When ready to serve, they should be brought back to temperature on the stove over low heat and finished by stirring in the mascarpone and seasoning with salt and pepper to taste.

FOR THE OYSTER STEW:
- 1 TABLESPOON PLUGRÁ® UNSALTED BUTTER
- ½ GARLIC CLOVE, MINCED
- 1 MEDIUM SHALLOT, DICED
- ½ RED BELL PEPPER, DICED
- ½ YELLOW BELL PEPPER, DICED
- ½ GREEN BELL PEPPER, DICED
- 1 CUP SEASONAL MUSHROOMS, CLEANED AND SLICED
- 1 PINT SHUCKED CHESAPEAKE BAY OYSTERS AND THEIR LIQUOR

- 1 CUP DEMI-GLACE
- ½ TO 1 TABLESPOON COARSELY GROUND BLACK PEPPER
- 4 SLICES APPLE-WOOD SMOKED BACON, DICED, COOKED, AND DRAINED
- 4 TABLESPOONS HEAVY CREAM
- 2 TABLESPOONS CHOPPED FRESH HERBS (PARSLEY, CHERVIL, TARRAGON, AND/OR CHIVES)
- KOSHER SALT
- CRISPY POTATO GAUFRETTES (WAFFLE CHIPS), FOR GARNISH

MELT THE BUTTER in a large sauté pan over medium heat. Add the garlic and shallots and sauté until just fragrant. Add the peppers and mushrooms and sauté until the vegetables are soft. Deglaze the pan with the natural juices the oysters are packed in (their "liquor"). Then add the demi-glace and the coarsely ground pepper to taste. Bring the mixture to a simmer. Stir in the bacon. When ready to serve, add the whole oysters and poach them in the simmering "stew" just until the edges of the oyster begin to become ruffled, about 30 seconds. Stir in the cream, the herbs, and season with salt to taste.

To serve, place a generous serving of grits in each bowl. Ladle the stew over the grits. Garnish each bowl with a gaufrette (crispy potato waffle chip).

FERMENTED
HOT SAUCE

APPROXIMATELY
1 16OZ MASON JAR

The base of this spicy sauce is made from fresh hot chile peppers. I recommend using an assortment rather than just one kind. Some of my favorite varieties to use are Espelette, Aji Dulce, Habanero, Scotch Bonnet, Tabasco, Serrano, and Thai. You will want the reddest chilies you can find as they will be the most ripe and will contain the most natural sugars. These sugars are what the yeast feeds on while the sauce ferments.

When chopping the chilies, be sure to leave all the seeds as that's where all the heat lives. If you prefer a milder hot sauce, then it's ok to remove the seeds. And ... be sure you wear gloves when handling these extra spicy chilies. I promise, you will thank me!

FOR THE FERMENTATION PROCESS:
- 1 POUND FRESH HOT CHILE PEPPERS
- 1 ½ TABLESPOONS KOSHER SALT

CUT OFF THE STEMS of all the chilies. Rough chop the chilies into small pieces and put them into a mixing bowl. Sprinkle the salt over the chilies and mash them up real good to start releasing their juices. Transfer the chilies and all their juices into a 16-ounce Mason jar and cover with a piece of cheesecloth. (A coffee filter will also work.) Then screw the band of the Mason jar lid down on the jar so that air can still flow through the cheesecloth. Place the jar somewhere you will see it daily in your kitchen activities.

A harmless, natural white mold will begin to form on the surface of the chilies. Scrape the mold off gently, being careful to not to let it go into the chilies mixture. Discard the mold. With a different spoon, stir the remaining ingredients a couple of times and then cover again the cheesecloth lid.

After the first week, you will start to see bubbles forming and you will know you have a great fermentation going. Repeat this scraping off of the mold about every 2 weeks. Let this continue until the bubbles stop (approximately 4 to 6 weeks).

FOR THE HOT SAUCE:
- ½ TO 1 CUP DISTILLED WHITE VINEGAR

ONCE THE FERMENTATION process has stopped and the final mold (if any) has been scraped off and discarded, puree the contents of the jar in a blender until completely smooth.

Measure the volume of the puree. Add half that amount of vinegar. Stir to combine.

Taste and check the seasoning. It is not likely you will need any more salt, but adjust to your liking. Place the hot sauce in a clean Mason jar, cover tightly with the Mason jar lid, and store in the refrigerator until ready to use.

PIMIENTO CHEESE

SERVES 4 TO 6

Pimiento cheese is the perfect boat snack. I like to throw some in a deli container, grab a box of crackers ... and we have a really easy and really wonderful snack.

When making pimiento cheese, it is really important to have a really good mayonnaise and really good cheese. I always use Duke's® mayonnaise. It's a wonderful product from here in Richmond and it has been my go-to mayo forever.

Using a really high quality cheddar is also important. At the restaurant, I use Grafton cheddar from Vermont. It's an aged cheddar that's not too sharp and has a real depth of flavor.

When it comes to seasoning your pimiento cheese, add more or less smoked paprika and Sriracha sauce depending on how smoky and/or spicy you would like it.

- 2/3 CUP DUKE'S® MAYONNAISE
- 1/3 CUP SOUR CREAM
- ¼ CUP CREAM CHEESE, SOFTENED
- 1 TEASPOON GRANULATED SUGAR
- 2 CUPS GRAFTON CHEDDAR, GRATED (OR ANY SHARP, WHITE CHEDDAR WILL WORK)
- ¾ CUP SMOKED GOUDA, GRATED
- ¾ CUP PIQUILLO PEPPERS, FINELY DICED
- ½ CUP PEPPADEW PEPPERS, FINELY DICED
- 2 GARLIC CLOVES, MINCED
- 1 SHALLOT (SMALL), MINCED
- 3 TEASPOONS SMOKED PAPRIKA
- 1 ½ TEASPOON SRIRACHA SAUCE (OR YOUR FAVORITE HOT CHILI SAUCE)
- KOSHER SALT AND FRESHLY GROUND BLACK PEPPER

IN A LARGE MIXING BOWL, stir together the mayonnaise, sour cream, cream cheese, and sugar until smooth. Add the cheddar, gouda, the peppers, garlic, and shallots. Stir, mashing with a fork, until well combined. Stir in the smoked paprika and Sriracha. Season with salt and pepper to taste. Cover and refrigerate until ready to serve.

"That's my church—the ocean, the bay, and the rivers. It's a beauty I cannot describe. I am at complete peace on the water. It is a special place and feeling for me. It's like what I would imagine heaven to be."

JOHN CURRENCE

FISHERMEN: John Currence | Richard Currence | Billy Reid
FISHING GUIDES: Nash Roberts IV | Nash Roberts III

PORT
SULPHUR, LA

HERE'S THE DEFINITION OF IRONY:
I don't give a shit about fishing,
but there is nowhere in the world
that I would rather be than in a
boat in the south Louisiana marsh,
hauling in speckled trout and
redfish. The irony is that the two
are not mutually exclusive.

JOHN CURRENCE
OXFORD, MS

Currence is executive chef and
owner of City Grocery, opened
1992, and City Restaurant
Group, which now includes
Nacho Mama's, Kalo's, Ajax
Diner, City Grocery Catering
Company, Bouré, Big Bad
Breakfast and Snackbar.
Southern Foodways Alliance
Guardian of Tradition Award,
2006. The Great American
Seafood Cookoff, New
Orleans, 2008. James Beard
Foundation Best Chef South
and winner of Charleston Food
and Wine Festival's Iron Chef
Challenge, 2009, and multiple
nominations from the James
Beard Foundation. Books
include *Pickles, Pigs & Whiskey:
Recipes from My Three Favorite
Food Groups and Then Some*
(Andrews McMeel Publishing,
2013) and *Big Bad Breakfast*
(Ten Speed Press, 2016).
Contributing editor at *Garden
& Gun* magazine.

I HAVE NO PATIENCE for the nuances involved in bass fishing, creeping silently around pond edges and tossing bait carefully between fallen trees, nor have I ever had the interest in learning the subtle cadence and flow of fly fishing. I guess I love to "fish," but have no time for "angling," simply put.

Depending on wind, tide, weather, and a fistful of other factors, the water around the mouth of the Mississippi River can vary from a murky brown to a Caribbean crystal clear. It is on those days when the gods of clarity conspire in your favor on a rising or falling tide that you want to know the exact cut in the marsh because you can haul in speckled trout as fast as you can put a shrimp on a hook and put it into the water. There is nothing like those days. They are the days fishing is furious and short-lived and you're going to, more often than not, put fish in the box and be back at the dock for a late breakfast before morning is done. It's beautiful.

Striking out from New Orleans to fish the mouth of the Mississippi River, where I have done most of my life's catching, mornings begin early. It's an hour-and-a-half drive and you want to be on the water at sunrise. There is little more beautiful than watching the sun crawl above the marsh grass. It bathes you in warmth and immediately tests the endurance of your eyes. A briny smell rises from the marsh grass as the world wakes and birds take flight. Shrimp trawlers and impossibly flat oyster boats chug along through the marsh water as we head out. They belch diesel exhaust and sag under the weight of nets and rigging. Everything about them looks as exhausted as their work implies. The wooden dreadnaughts of the shallows have been chipped; sanded and repainted enough times they look to be made of alligator skin, rather than cypress. The marsh is a gold mine for what they seek.

The water glistens like a field of a billion diamonds. When the sun is out, it is unforgiving on the retinas. It plays tricks on you. It winks. It grins. It hypnotizes with impossible images dancing in that light. Hundreds of horsepower scream like demons from the Mercury outboard that carries us skittering across an expanse of bronze salt water, diluted slightly by the Mississippi River's final breath.

Skipping across the tops of sculpture-esque oyster beds and long-running mud flats, Nash Roberts IV rarely says a word. His ruddy skin and calloused hands tell the tale of a man who spends, on average, 200 days a year on the water. His raccoon's tan from his wraparound sunglasses and a softness to his eyes belie the harshness of his surroundings.

Fishing guides are a little like basketball coaches, in my experience. They say little as they scan the expanse for opportunity. They can seem terse in their response because they speak so infrequently and when they do, they stab at their words with economy and conviction. When they find fish, though, they are immediately animated and become a torrential waterfall of urgency, clearing the decks, checking the Shimano reels for drag tension, setting baits, adjusting the electric trolling motors, and readying nets, all while keeping their eyes on the water. Fish are as much the enemy as the prize.

For Nash, it is an effortless routine, like Sinatra pulling out a cigarette and lighting it, when most other men would look as clumsy as a newborn colt trying to accomplish the same task. It is just an extension of his being. He is the consummate professional and the best at what he does on the waters of south Louisiana. We have fished together for more than 25 years and I cannot think of a time that Nash hasn't put us on top of fish.

He is easy to like. His grandfather, for whom he is named (as was his father), was the Walter Cronkite of New Orleans. For decades he delivered remarkably accurate weather reports from one of the local TV stations. He was as beloved and respected as anyone in the city...a city built on the principles of *laissez faire*, New Orleans never really entertained celebrity, but Nash Jr. was an exception. Nash IV possesses many of the same qualities as his grandfather (and father, for that matter). He is exceptional at his chosen field. He is focused and extremely dedicated, yet approachable and inordinately kind. He is wise and loves sharing what he has learned about his craft. His patience knows no bounds and he truly looks upon every man as "everyman." He is, above all, a gentleman.

My dad is particularly fond of Nash. They share a mutual respect for each other's love of the sport. They are both men of few words. Both are disgustingly punctual, fastidious, and organized. Each is thoughtful and they just like spending time together, which explains why I wasn't as shocked as most normal people might have been when I walked into my folks' house and saw Nash's wedding picture in their living room the first time. Yep, that happened. Not me...or my brother...but Nash and Elizabeth. It tickles me every time I see it. In all fairness, he is married to a close friend of the family, but he is just that endearing and Dad is just that weird.

Evenings around our house, as a child, were pretty scripted. Mom taught school, so we all came home together. My brother and I played outside in the afternoons while mom cooked supper, graded tests, and did lesson plans. We came in about the time Dad got home, in time to make a glass of Johnnie Walker and watch the news before dinner. On occasion, Dad would turn his attention to me to share a gem of knowledge or offer an observation I was invariably far too young to truly understand. In 1974, as Nixon was coming completely apart, I remember my dad squaring up my shoulders and looking at him, red-faced, as another day's news about the impeachment proceedings passed. He began to bellow at me about Nixon's undoing. "Son, you are watching the unwarranted dismantling of a great American president. These dumb sons-of-bitches on his staff are taking him down. Remember: You are only ever as good as the people you surround yourself with," he roared. It was a lesson I would remember that would come in handy later, whether in my business or writing.

Shortly after this, Dad's company sent us to Edinburgh, Scotland, for several years. Dad was in the tugboat business. His tugs and supply boats provided support to offshore drilling efforts and in the early 1970's there was a spike in drilling activity in the North Sea. That office had served as little more than a dispatch and supply depot for a couple of boats stationed in the area. Within a matter of months after Dad's arrival, it would become a bustling international headquarters for his company's growing worldwide business.

Not only was there enough activity in the North Sea to merit moving a significant portion of his company's fleet to the area, business began to bubble up in western Africa, Egypt, India, and beyond. And Dad was a one-man show.

Short of help and with a tornado of business whirling around him, he began plucking his best captains from their boats and turning them into operations managers. Dad put together a band of pirates to run what was the international gateway office for his company.

Dad's two closest confidants were Hugh "Mutt" Miller, a quiet but hard country boy from Picayune, Mississippi, and Tommy Sheridan, a west Texas gentle giant who had worked as a guard in the Texas prison system before becoming a boat captain. Like Dad, these were not men of refined upbringing nor had any of them been anywhere near a business school. They just all knew the business of boats and they all loved to work and excel.

Dad's reputation for keen negotiating skills, ability to adapt to his surroundings, find work for his boats and as an industry clairvoyant began in these years. He was enormously respected by his peers in the business community, and was successful because he understood the significance of the wisdom of the guys he built his team with while still taking cues from other executives in the industry. In short order, he became the most respected man in the world at what he did. Dad had an air of confidence when it came to his work, but arrogance was a trait he never displayed.

Billy Reid and I got to know each other some twelve years ago. He had taken an interest in the work of the Southern Foodways Alliance (SFA). I was intrigued with why this budding men's clothing designer was attracted to the work of a focused academic food organization and why he was interested in becoming a financial benefactor to the group. I quickly learned that Billy, whose star was ascending rapidly in the fashion industry (he famously warmed the chilly heart of Anna Wintour), had built his successes with a team in his chosen headquarters in his wife's hometown of Florence, Alabama. Like the SFA, Billy was dedicated to selling authenticity in his work, celebrating the quality and significance of people contributing to his field, and harvesting and preserving stories and history of our culture that might otherwise get lost without deliberate curators. We are all people who care about and deeply love our "place."

Billy first launched his brand from Dallas in 2001, only to see his dream stalled by the attacks and economic downturn of 9/11. Determined to see his vision through, he set up shop in Florence, employing in-laws and locals who wanted to learn his vision for style, quality, and service. In a town that could not be more removed from the fashion capitals of New York, Paris, and Milan philosophically, if not geographically, Billy built his team. And they were brilliant. Carpenters became models for his early shoots, sisters-in-law became retail managers, and friends became consultants. I immediately wanted in.

Having both been reared in south Louisiana with similar values and vision, it didn't take much to kindle a friendship, but it was Billy's dedication to giving himself to whatever community he was invested in that I admired most deeply. Whether he was opening a store in Charleston, South Carolina, coaching Little League baseball or participating with the SFA, Billy was all-in. He is a man who seeks excellence, recognizes quality, values relationships, and gives uncontrollably. He loves whiskey, good food, family, hunting, fishing, and SEC football, among other things. He is entirely unimpressed with celebrity, but speechless, at times, faced with true character. He is at once himself, a character but unfailingly genuine. He is wise, but entirely approachable. He is a man's man and someone you hope will remember your name. More often than not, he will.

Billy's friends' causes become Billy's causes by default. I don't think it was long into our very first conversation, shortly after hurricane Katrina, when I was talking about a rebuilding project I was helming in New Orleans. In mid-sentence, he demanded that should we need anything he could provide, to let him know. In the last decade, we have jumped in for each other wherever the need lay. I have cooked dinners in his home and stores for auctions and charity events on more occasions than I can recall and he has offered clothing, baseball caps, and custom-tailored suits for our charities. "No" is not a big part of his vocabulary...I don't think I have ever heard it uttered.

In 2014, I partnered with friends at Yalobusha Brewing Company to make a beer that I wanted to drink. I could not be more bored with the current trend in craft beers. Simply put, I don't like things that are overtly bitter. Combine that with the fact that I just don't see the need to intellectualize beer and, well, there it is...I just don't give a crap. I am, however, fascinated with the process and the craft itself, which led me to the question, "if Budweiser is the best-selling beer in the world and craft beer makers think it is shitty AND they all want to make the new best beer ever, then why not make a better Budweiser?" So we did.

Proceeds from the sale of our beer feed directly into our non-profit foundation, Move On Up Mississippi, which funds existing programs in the state that work in the areas of childhood health, well-being, and education. The moment the beer was available for sale in New Orleans, Billy called insisting he host an event in his local store. We packed his little store with friends and family, all keenly interested in the foundation. It was a perfect moment. We kissed the cheeks of old friends and embraced new, thanks to Billy's kindness.

As a way of saying "thank you," I enlisted Nash to take my brother Richard, Billy, and me fishing that morning.

Richard is the embodiment of some of our father's finest qualities. He possesses all of Dad's business acumen, forthrightness, and honesty and is one of the best dads I know. He is unfailingly funny, whip-smart, resolute, and sedulous. There are few people on the planet I prefer spending time with. There is nobody I love fishing with more.

I do not and never have played matchmaker, but there are certain times when people in my life should get to know each other because I am sure they will enrich themselves through their association. These three men boarded Nash's boat that morning as strangers to disembark as friends. And those friendships may have never been cemented anywhere else than on Nash's boat. A day spent in the marsh can blur the lines that normally separate people, providing an opportunity to recapture a moment lost in a busy world, a chance to unplug, a chance to stare the beauty of nature in the eye, and a chance to spend uninterrupted time with people you love.

"A designer, a businessman, a chef, and the grandson of a weatherman get on a boat," sounds like the setup for a joke. And while on this boat, on this day, there were most definitely comedians, and there were three of the finest men I know. All three are products of their upbringing, all three are outstanding in their individual fields, and all three are from completely different backgrounds.

Nash's boat allows us to escape ourselves and connect as nothing more than residents of the same planet with similar concerns, joys, and values. It is a place of peace. It is a place of serenity. Simply said, it is a place where we all need to spend a little more time.

Thank you, Nash. ✼

"'A designer, a businessman, a chef and the grandson of a weatherman get on a boat,' sounds like the setup for a joke. And while on this boat, on this day, there were most definitely comedians, and there were three of the finest men I know."

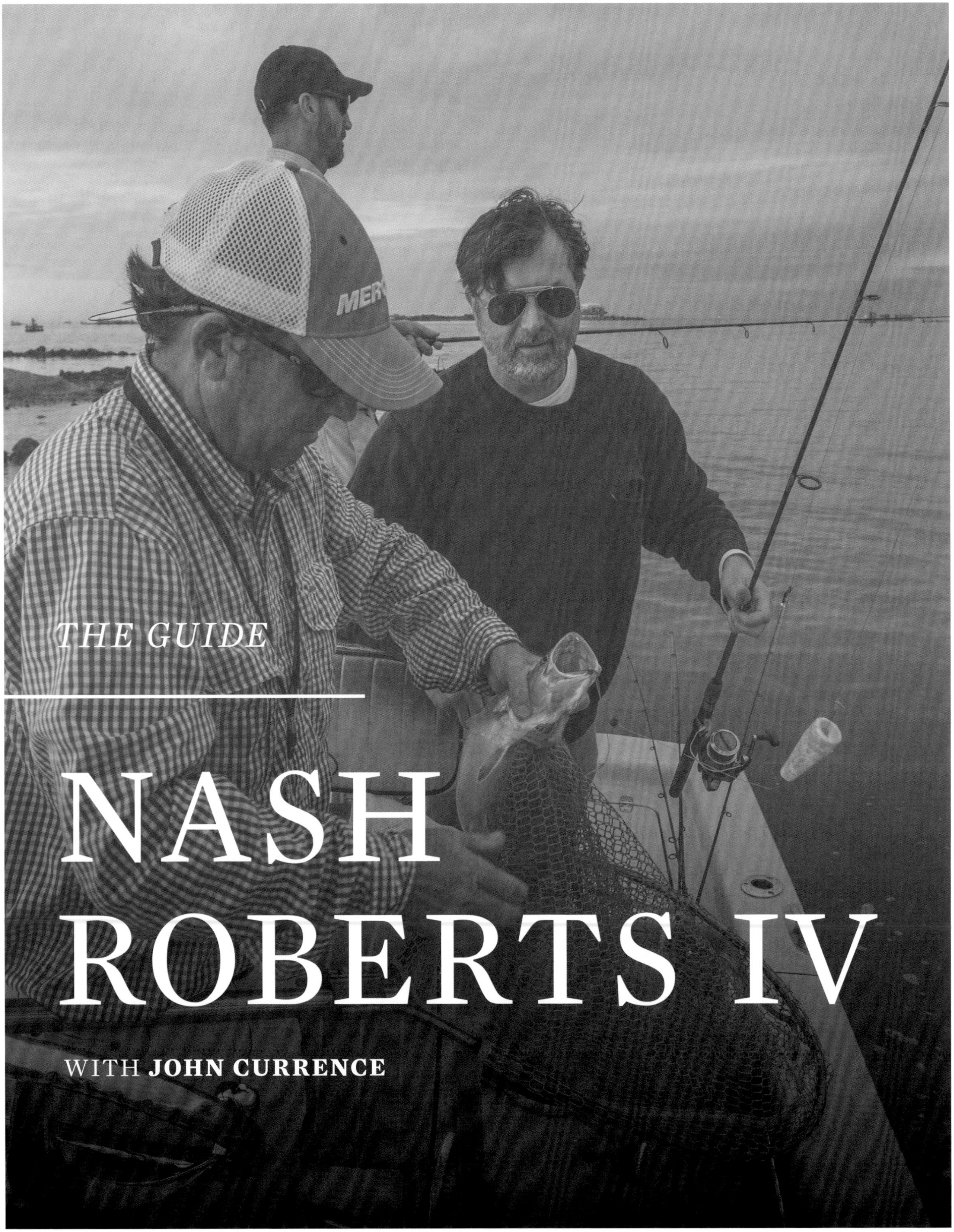

THE GUIDE

NASH ROBERTS IV

WITH **JOHN CURRENCE**

NASH ROBERTS IV is part of a father/son guide duo. Both Nash III and Nash IV are degreed biologists and full-time fishing guides based near Port Sulphur, Louisiana, about 50 minutes southeast of New Orleans in the heart of the best redfishing in the United States. They operate from a private fishing camp, surrounded by a pristine, shallow-water coastal marsh that extends as far as the eye can see. "Shallow-water redfishing in water less than two feet in depth is our specialty. We generally employ bass fishing techniques, casting spoons, spinners, jigs, and top-water baits to the edges of marsh islands and over oyster reefs."

REDFISH are the top of the food chain in the marsh; they eat most everything and nothing eats them. This leads to an aggressive behavior that results in rod-jarring strikes and explosive action!

Prime time to fish reds is August through March. Moderate winter temperatures in the marsh make for a pleasant escape from the sometimes bitter cold over much of the nation during the best redfishing season. Redfish average 4 to 8 pounds during this period, but trophy or bull reds that range from 25 to 40 pounds are targeted in March and September.

I've become a speckled trout specialist, too, over the years. At least half my customers want to catch nice speckled trout—15 inches and up. Personally, I don't consider a trout a trophy until it is over five pounds.

I enjoy shallow-water fishing in particular because I love to watch fish eat. Trout are one of the best-eating fish. When you are on them, you can catch a bunch. They are aggressive and will take top-water baits. They are more of a challenge than redfish because they are so susceptible to the weather. The weather is everything on trout. You can have the best tide in the world, but if it's blowing 20 miles an hour, trout fishing is tough. When you get the right conditions, it's heaven.

"Proceeds from the sale of our beer feed directly into our non-profit foundation, Move On Up Mississippi, which funds existing programs in the state that do work in the areas of childhood health, well-being and education. The moment the beer was available for sale in New Orleans, Billy called insisting he host an event in his local store. We packed his little store with friends and family, all keenly interested in the foundation and hoping to support our work. It was a perfect moment. We kissed the cheeks of old friends and embraced new, thanks to Billy's kindness."

SMOKED TROUT DIP

SERVES 6 TO 8

When we went to the beach on the panhandle of Florida when I was a kid, Smoked Mullet Dip was a fridge stable. It always came out at Happy Hour ... which was basically the entire time we were at the beach!

I was always amazed at how someone could take something as stinky as the mullet smelled on the boat and transform it into something as delicious as Smoked Mullet Dip.

The jump to using smoked trout was not a stroke of brilliance as much as a lateral move. Trout is delicious as it is, so the addition of mayonnaise (a universal healer, even though you mayo-haters out there refuse to understand) moves that protein into the realm of transcendent.

- 1/3 CUP SOUR CREAM
- 1/3 CUP MAYONNAISE
- 1 1/2 TABLESPOONS DIJON MUSTARD
- 1 TABLESPOON PREPARED HORSERADISH
- 2 TABLESPOONS CHOPPED FRESH CHIVES
- ZEST AND JUICE OF 1 LEMON
- 1 TEASPOON OLD BAY® SEASONING
- 1/4 CUP GRATED YELLOW ONION
- 1 POUND SMOKED TROUT, FLAKED INTO SMALL PIECES
- KOSHER SALT AND FRESHLY GROUND BLACK PEPPER
- TABASCO®

IN A LARGE BOWL, stir together the sour cream, mayonnaise, mustard, horseradish, chives, lemon zest and juice, Old Bay® Seasoning, and the onion until well blended.

Add the flaked trout and stir until well combined. Season with salt, pepper, and Tabasco® to taste.

TROUT TACOS

MAKES 12 TACOS

In 2005, I took a motorcycle trip with one of my best friends down into Mexico on the Baja Peninsula for about a week. We jumped from town to town drinking tequila and beer mostly, but managed to find some unbelievable food on the streets.

One of those stops was a little roadside shack outside of Ensenada that served fish tacos ... and only fish tacos.

We had taken an insane ride that had taken us from the warm desert on the east side of the peninsula, through ice and snow in the mountains, and down into the coastal climate in Ensenada. The ride was harrowing. The fish tacos and ice cold Modelo™ that came along with them could not have hit the spot any better.

Trout fries up so nicely ... and these tacos take me back to Ensenada every time I make them.

- 1 POUND FRESH TROUT, CUT INTO 1/2 INCH SLIVERS
- KOSHER SALT AND FRESHLY GROUND BLACK PEPPER
- 5 CUPS ALL-PURPOSE FLOUR, DIVIDED
- 2 CUPS CORNMEAL
- 1/2 TEASPOON CAYENNE PEPPER
- 1 1/2 TEASPOONS GROUND CUMIN
- 1 TEASPOON GROUND CORIANDER
- 4 LARGE EGGS
- 1/2 CUP MILK
- 1/2 CUP MAYONNAISE
- ZEST AND JUICE OF 1 LIME
- 2 TABLESPOONS MINCED JALAPEÑO PEPPERS
- 2 TABLESPOONS CHOPPED FRESH CILANTRO
- VEGETABLE OIL FOR FRYING
- 12 SMALL CORN TORTILLAS
- 2 CUPS SHREDDED LETTUCE
- 1 CUP FRESH PICO DE GALLO
- VALENTINA™ HOT SAUCE
- LIME WEDGES

PAT THE FISH dry and season with salt and pepper.

In one shallow bowl, season 3 cups of flour lightly with salt and pepper. In another shallow bowl, blend the remaining flour with the cornmeal and season with salt and pepper as well. Stir in the cayenne, cumin, and coriander. In a third shallow bowl, stir together the eggs and milk and season with salt and pepper.

In a small bowl, stir together the mayonnaise, lime zest and juice, minced jalapeños, and chopped cilantro until well-combined. Cover and refrigerate until ready to serve.

Warm 1 1/2 inches of vegetable oil in a skillet to 375°F.

Dredge the fish first in the seasoned flour, then the egg wash, and then finally in the cornmeal.

In batches so as not to over crowd the skillet, fry the fish for 2 to 3 minutes, or until golden brown. Using a slotted spoon, transfer the fish to a paper towel-lined plate to drain.

Spoon a little bit of the fry oil into a second pan, just to barely coat the bottom. Warm the pan over medium-high heat. Fry the tortillas in batches of 2 or 3 until they get a little color, but are not crispy.

Spread the sauce on each tortilla, top with the fish, lettuce, pico de gallo, and hot sauce. Serve with lime wedges. Eat immediately.

ENGLISH PEA VELOUTÉ

SERVES 12

This is absolutely sick with fresh English peas in early spring time. You can serve it hot or cold.

Topped with flaked broiled trout, crème fraîche, and fresh herbs, it is unbeatable. And ... for the record, it is just as good with crabmeat, sautéed shrimp, or seared scallops.

FOR THE TROUT:

- 2 MEDIUM TROUT FILETS
- 1/4 CUP EXTRA-VIRGIN OLIVE OIL
- KOSHER SALT
- WHITE PEPPER

PREHEAT the broiler to high.

Rub the trout filets with the olive oil and lightly season with salt and pepper. Place the trout on a baking sheet and roast under the broiler for 4 minutes, or until nicely browned. Remove from the oven, let cool, and flake into small pieces.

FOR THE VELOUTÉ:

- 2 3/4 CUPS BUTTER, DIVIDED
- 2 CUPS ALL-PURPOSE FLOUR
- 1 1/2 CUPS MINCED SHALLOTS
- 3 TABLESPOONS MINCED GARLIC
- 2 CUPS MINCED CELERY
- 4 POUNDS ENGLISH PEAS
- 3 TABLESPOONS FRESH THYME LEAVES
- 3 CUPS DRY WHITE WINE
- 12 CUPS CHICKEN STOCK
- 1/2 CUP FRESH MINT LEAVES, ROUGHLY TORN
- KOSHER SALT
- WHITE PEPPER
- 1 1/2 CUPS CRÈME FRAÎCHE
- 2 TABLESPOONS CHOPPED FRESH HERBS (ANY BLEND WILL BE FINE)

START BY MAKING a blonde roux. Melt 2 cups of the butter in a saucepan over medium heat. Stir in the flour and cook for 15 to 20 minutes, stirring constantly, until a light golden color. Set the roux aside.

In soup pot, melt the remaining 3/4 cup butter over medium-high heat. Add the shallot, garlic, and celery and sauté until transparent. Add the peas and thyme and sauté on high for 7 to 8 minutes.

Deglaze with the white wine. Add the chicken stock and bring the mixture to a boil. Simmer for 5 minutes and then stir in 3/4 of the roux. Bring to a simmer again.

Puree the mixture with an immersion blender and stir in 1 cup crème fraîche and the mint. Puree a little more once the mint leaves have started to wilt. Season with salt and white pepper to taste.

To serve, divide the velouté into bowls and top with the remaining crème fraîche, flaked trout, fresh herbs, and a drizzle of extra virgin olive oil.

TROUT SALAD LARDON

SERVES 2

One of the finest salads I ever ate in my life came served with a massive dose of heartbreak. I was a melodramatic young man and the morning after having my chubby little heart crushed, I soldiered on alone on a trip for Paris that was supposed to be for two. By the time I arrived in Paris, my anger had morphed into agony.

A family friend picked me up from Charles de Gaulle airport and whisked me into the countryside. In the courtyard of this beautiful (and what could not have looked any more cliché) little restaurant, I was served a PERFECT salad lardon with poached scallops. I have chased that unicorn ever since. This is my homage to that salad ... and my middle finger to that girl.

FOR THE LARDONS:
- 1/4 POUND SLAB BACON
- 1 TABLESPOON OLIVE OIL

CUT THE BACON into 1/4-inch cubes and fry over medium heat in the olive oil until browned and crispy on the outside. Transfer to a paper towel-lined plate to drain.

FOR THE VINAIGRETTE:
- 1/4 CUP + 2 TABLESPOONS OLIVE OIL
- 3 TABLESPOONS CHAMPAGNE VINEGAR
- ZEST AND JUICE OF 1 LEMON
- 1 1/2 TABLESPOONS CHOPPED FRESH HERBS (ANY MIXTURE WILL DO)
- 1 TABLESPOON GRAINY MUSTARD
- 1 TABLESPOON MINCED SHALLOTS
- 1 TEASPOON SUGAR
- KOSHER SALT AND FRESHLY GROUND BLACK PEPPER

IN A BOWL, whisk together all the ingredients for the vinaigrette. Season with salt and pepper. Set aside until ready to serve.

FOR THE TROUT:
- 2 TROUT FILLETS (4-OUNCES EACH)
- KOSHER SALT AND FRESHLY GROUND BLACK PEPPER
- 1/2 CUP ALL-PURPOSE FLOUR
- 3 TABLESPOONS CLARIFIED BUTTER

LIGHTLY SEASON the trout with salt and pepper. Lightly dredge through the flour, shaking off any excess.

Warm the clarified butter in a skillet over medium-high heat. Add the trout and cook for 3 minutes on each side. Remove the trout from the heat.

FOR THE SALAD:
- 2 LARGE HANDFULS FRISÉE
- 2 TABLESPOONS MINCED SHALLOTS
- 1 1/2 CUPS CROUTONS
- 2 RADISHES, SLIVERED
- 1/4 CUP GRATED FRESH BEET
- 2 LIGHTLY POACHED EGGS

TOSS ALL the salad ingredients (except the eggs) together in a large bowl. Drizzle with half the vinaigrette and toss again, seasoning with salt and black pepper to taste.

Divide the salad evenly between two plates. Sprinkle a small handful of the lardons on each salad. Top with a trout fillet and an egg. Drizzle a little of the remaining vinaigrette over the egg and trout.

KELLY ENGLISH

FISHERMEN: Kelly English | Luke Ehrensing
Jonathan Jones | Ryan Plummer | Andy Rice | Lee Smith
FISHING GUIDE: Don Helmer
RESCUE BOAT CAPTAIN: Ike Truehill

VENICE, LA

EVERYONE HAS THAT "THING" that centers them. Some people do things in groups, some people like to be alone, some people like silence, and others need some noise. I need all of that, and getting back a little south of where I grew up, to Venice, Louisiana, is where I get it.

KELLY ENGLISH
MEMPHIS, TN

English is executive chef and owner of Restaurant Iris, The Second Line, Memphis, The Second Line, Oxford, MS, and Iris Etc. Catering Services in Memphis and is executive chef at Magnolia House, Biloxi, MS. He was named a James Beard Award Semifinalist for Best Chef Southeast in 2009, and has appeared on the Food Network. In February 2012, English was named Memphis' "Prince of Porc" in the national Cochon555 competition, which landed him a seat at the 2012 Aspen Food & Wine Festival. English has been featured in *Food & Wine* magazine, *Everyday with Rachael Ray*, *Bon Appétit*, *Garden & Gun*, and the cookbook *Wild Abundance*.

YOU SEE, fishing in the gulf has all of that: the roar of the boat coupled with the silence when at rest, fishing with a group of people who don't get to see each other enough peppered with moments that are just you and a few pelicans. Fishing in Venice, Louisiana, never changes, save for a touch of water sport innovation over the years or a disaster, either man-made or natural (but that is a different book). My good friend Luke Ehrensing had a barge that was anchored in the Breton Sound that we used to go to before Katrina. She decided she wanted that barge, so now he has one that he keeps in Venice proper. It is my favorite phone call, when he invites a few people down for a weekend.

The drive down is like hitting rewind on the VHS tape of my life, straight down I-55. Pull out of my adopted hometown of Memphis, and head south past the exit to Oxford in Mississippi where I learned so much about who I wanted to be, and almost as importantly, did not want to be. Keep going straight through Hammond, Louisiana, where you can turn right on to I-12 to Baton Rouge, where I spent my last two years of high school, or turn left to go see my parents in Mandeville. Due south still is New Orleans, where I did most of my growing up. Pass through and head to Venice.

As usual, I ride from New Orleans with my buddy Ryan Plummer, who, outside of my chef friends, is the guy who is the most passionate about food I know anywhere. He makes what most people call a "killer frickin ceviche" that we are having tomorrow.

When we get to Venice we are greeted by Don Helmer, a man that has been around salt water his whole life. All you need to do is look him in the eye and hear him talk to know that.

Getting back down here always means a few things to me.
First, no matter how much I make Memphis my home,
I always miss being that close to the ocean. It always
calms me. Spending time with a few people who I would
do anything for and who would do anything for me is
something that nobody in my profession does enough. I'm
always reminded of why I became a chef: It is right there
watching my friends who don't do this for a living paying
attention to details as if they did. It also reminds me of
where I came from, fishing the same water that I did with
my dad as a kid. If I become a dad one day I hope to bring
my son or daughter down here, too.

Life is all about moments ... you add them up at the
end and see what you made of them. There are lots of
moments that go by too quickly, then there are moments
when time stands still. The thing about fishing in
Venice is that both happen simultaneously. When I add
everything up, these trips have their own column. ❀

"My favorite places to fish
are near the old oil rigs that
aren't in use anymore, as
much for the fish as to take
in just how big the gulf is."

"Life is all about moments ... you add them up at the end and see what you made of them. There are lots of moments that go by too quickly, then there are moments when time stands still. The thing about fishing in Venice is that both happen simultaneously. When I add everything up, these trips have their own column."

THE GUIDE

DON
HELMER

WITH **KELLY ENGLISH**

Our first dinner is at the restaurant a few steps away from the barge. Admittedly this dinner is more about the liquids than the solids, but who's keeping score? It isn't often I get some of my favorite people — Luke, Ryan, Jonathan Jones, Lee Smith, and Andy Rice — around a table. We stay there a little too late and then we head back to the barge. The guys with children at home usually go to sleep, and the guys who don't stay up a bit later. Call it reverse natural selection.

Waking up the next morning is never hard. Don has the boat and gear ready to go; all you need is sunscreen and a few ham sandwiches to go along with a full cooler. We ride out for a bit and then it's all redfish or speckled trout and a few sharks.

My favorite places to fish are near the old oil rigs that aren't in use anymore, as much for the fish as to take in just how big the gulf is. That moment when you are kind of by yourself while being surrounded with people you love … that's the perfect place and time to me. It doesn't matter what boat you are on with what pole, you get that moment every time no matter what.

When we start making our way back, the attention naturally turns to cooking some of what we just caught, and when we arrive we all have a role. The one constant is Don's redfish on the half shell. First you need a big fish. Slap it down and filet it leaving the skin and scales on, add a little salt and whatever seasoning you like, a little lemon and butter, and grill it scale-side down until it is done.

Ryan is at the dining room table getting his ceviche together. Lee is getting our favorite snack together, which was always Pickapeppa on cream cheese until he started making his own stuff with his brother Joe. I am working on a tomato and crab salad and a court bouillon with red drum, oysters, and crabs we caught in a trap on the way in. One of the things I love about this trip is that we eat everything out of this one body of water for dinner. I never understand when a restaurant near any body of salt water serves food from other parts of the world.

"That moment when you are kind of by yourself while being surrounded with people you love … that's the perfect place and time to me. It doesn't matter what boat you are on with what pole, you get that moment every time no matter what."

DON HELMER is a lifelong resident of Louisiana's bays and bayous. He grew up in Lafitte before moving to the sport fishing haven of Venice decades ago, where he works as both a fishing and hunting guide. His dad was a commercial fisherman, and as one of five kids, he says he just sort of followed along with everyone else. "I grew up on the water, and was just a kid when I did my first fishing, at 6 or 7 years old. I've been fishing all my life."

VENICE IS FAMOUS and is a top fishing destination because it's known for having the biggest variety of fish—sailfish, marlin, yellowfin tuna, cobia, redfish, speckled trout, and red snapper.

We head out to the old oil rigs, around 20 miles out, because we like to fish in deeper water, 14-18 feet deep. Redfish like the crabs and shrimp that hide around the old rig pipe and the barnacles that collect there, and the fish get bigger because there's more to eat. There are speckled trout in the same water.

We can also catch speckled trout in the open bay sometimes, or under a bridge. I watch for signs, if I see birds diving, I know there are speckled trout there, feeding on shrimp. Sometimes we fish closer but most of the time I like it offshore. There's less competition out there.

Some people like to fish towards the bank, and people do use artificial lures on the reefs that are closer inshore. But bigger fish are in a deeper place.

Early morning is the best time to fish, and in Venice, you want to fish on the incoming tide. When I fish offshore, the tide makes a difference. It's also good when the west wind is blowing away from the oil rigs. I use a Carolina rig with a 20-inch leader, and I use exclusively live bait ... shrimp and cocahoe minnows. May and June are the best season for redfish. July and August are still good for fishing, but it's hot.

I like fishing for all of them ... I'm not particular. Though I caught three cobia – ling—the other day. That's some good eatin'.

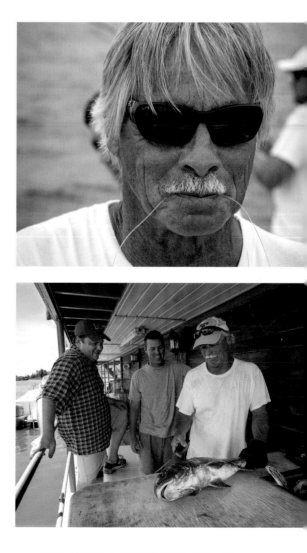

RYAN PLUMMER'S KILLER FRICKIN' CEVICHE

SERVES 12

I believe the name says it all.

My buddy Ryan Plummer, outside of my chef friends, is the guy that is the most passionate about food I know anywhere. He makes this ceviche every time our crew gets together for one of our Gulf fishing trips.

You can use most any fish you like ... but Ryan normally makes this with fish we catch out in the Gulf. Most often, it's snapper or red fish.

When making ceviche, it's key to let the fish marinate for just about 30 minutes. The acidic marinade actually "cooks" the fish. So if you don't leave it long enough, your fish will be raw and if you leave it too long, the fish will overcook and become tough.

FOR THE CEVICHE:

- 2 ½ POUNDS FRESH-CAUGHT FISH FILLETS, SKINNED AND DICED
- 1 ONION, MINCED
- 2 YELLOW BELL PEPPERS, FINELY DICED
- 1 AVOCADO, SLIGHTLY FIRMER THAN PERFECTLY RIPE, FINELY DICED
- 1 SERRANO PEPPER, ROASTED, SEEDED, AND DICED
- 2 JALAPEÑO PEPPERS, SEEDED AND DICED
- ½ CUP CHOPPED FRESH CILANTRO
- 8 LIMES, JUICED (IF SMALL LIMES USE MORE)
- 2 TABLESPOONS FISH SAUCE
- 3 TABLESPOONS SAMBAL OELEK
- ½ CUP OLIVE OIL
  KOSHER SALT AND FRESHLY GROUND BLACK PEPPER

PLACE ALL the ingredients in a bowl and toss to combine. Cover, refrigerate, and let marinate for about thirty minutes. Season with salt and pepper to taste.

TO FINISH THE DISH:

- 12 CRISPY CORN TOSTADA SHELLS
- 12 TEASPOONS MAYONNAISE
- 1 AVOCADO, TO SLICE ON TOP

SPREAD A TEASPOON of mayonnaise over each tostada shell, top with the ceviche, and then add a slice of avocado on top.

TOMATO AND CRAB SALAD WITH AVOCADO VINAIGRETTE

SERVES 12

This is my favorite thing to eat as soon as tomatoes hit their stride of the season. I like to use Creole tomatoes because they are the tomatoes I grew up eating in Louisiana. Creole tomatoes are very flavorful and juicy in their season, so find the best ones around where you are and use your local farmer.

Try this dish with poached shrimp as well, but nothing beats crabmeat for me.

FOR THE VINAIGRETTE:

- 1/3 CUP RICE WINE VINEGAR
- 1 CUP OLIVE OIL
- 1 TABLESPOON SRIRACHA SAUCE
- ½ BUNCH GREEN ONIONS, CHOPPED
- 1 RIPE AVOCADO, PEELED AND DICED
- KOSHER SALT AND FRESHLY GROUND BLACK PEPPER

IN A BOWL, whisk together the vinegar, oil, and Sriracha. Add the green onions and avocado and gently toss together. Season with salt and pepper to taste.

FOR THE SALAD:

- 3 NICE BIG RIPE TOMATOES, CUT INTO SLICES
- KOSHER SALT AND FRESHLY GROUND BLACK PEPPER
- 1 POUND FRESH GULF JUMBO LUMP CRAB, PICKED OF SHELLS

ARRANGE THE TOMATOES on a platter and season with salt and a generous amount of pepper. Top with the picked crabmeat and then spoon the vinaigrette on top. Serve immediately.

SMITH BROTHERS' PINEAPPLE-HABANERO DRIZZLE

MAKES 6 CUPS

My great friends Lee and Joe Smith make this spicy sauce and bring it everytime we get together. Most often, we serve this sweet and spicy concotion over cream cheese with wheat thins... or whatever cracker we have on hand. It's a tasty and easy-to-serve appertizer perfect for any occasion.

A staple in my kitchen, I always have it right next to the Pickapeppa Sauce that I use in exactly the same way.

Cooking Tip: *Lee and Joe always use Ball® RealFruit™ Classic Pectin. If you are using a different brand, you'll need to check your fruit/pepper/liquid to sugar ratio, which varies based on what brand of pectin you use.*

- 8 HABANERO PEPPERS, SEEDED AND DEVEINED
- 1 ORANGE BELL PEPPER, SEEDED AND DEVEINED
- 4 CUPS DICED FRESH PINEAPPLE
- 1 CUP VINEGAR
- 6 TABLESPOONS BALL® REALFRUIT™ CLASSIC PECTIN
- 5 CUPS SUGAR
- PINCH OF SALT

IN A BLENDER, process all of the peppers, pineapple, and vinegar until smooth.

Place the mixture in a saucepan with the pectin and bring to a boil. Stir in the sugar and a pinch of salt. Bring back to a boil and boil for about 2 to 3 more minutes, stirring frequently to prevent burning.

Ladle the hot mixture into sterilized canning jars, leaving 1/4-inch head room. Process the jars in a hot water bath.

VENICE COURT BOUILLON

SERVES 12

Fish stews are common around the Gulf Coast, but a Creole court bouillon (pronounced coo-bee-yon) is special. While it is related to the classic French technique (with the same spelling but different pronunciation) of gently poaching seafood in a delicate stock, it is also totally different. This downhome South Louisiana fish dish is a highly seasoned stew featuring tomatoes along with the holy trinity of vegetables and a good seafood stock.

I worked for a chef named Jared Tees at Lüke in New Orleans who cooked the best court bouillon I've ever had. This is my version of what he taught me.

Cooking Tip: *The key to making a blond roux is to cook the roux until it is just fragrant, but doesn't have color. I use equal parts flour and butter. For about 1 cup roux, melt 1 cup butter In a saucepan over medium heat. Whisk in 1 cup flour, 1 tablespoon at a time, and cook, whisking constantly, until the roux becomes a golden color.*

FOR THE SAUCE:
- ½ CUP CANOLA OIL
- 3 ONIONS, DICED
- 2 GREEN BELL PEPPERS, DICED
- ½ HEAD OF CELERY, DICED
- 4 GARLIC CLOVES, MINCED
- KOSHER SALT
- CAYENNE PEPPER
- 3 QUARTS SHRIMP STOCK (OR CHICKEN BROTH IF YOU CAN'T FIND IT)
- 1 CUP BLONDE ROUX
- 10 POUNDS RIPE TOMATOES, CHOPPED
- 1 BUNCH PARSLEY, ROUGHLY CHOPPED
- 1 BUNCH FRESH TARRAGON, ROUGHLY CHOPPED
- 2 BIG PINCHES GROUND ALLSPICE

HEAT THE CANOLA oil in a heavy-bottomed pot over medium-high heat. Add the onion, peppers, celery, and garlic and cook, stirring, until the vegetables have softened, about 10 minutes. Season with salt and cayenne pepper. Add the stock and bring to a simmer. Once at a full simmer, stir in the blonde roux. Cook for ten minutes over medium heat, stirring frequently. Add all the chopped tomatoes and bring to a simmer again. Stir in the parsley, tarragon, and allspice. Season with salt and cayenne pepper to taste. Let the sauce keep simmering while you sear the seafood.

FOR THE SEAFOOD:
- 6 BLUE CRABS, CUT IN HALF
- 6 SMALL REDFISH OR DRUM FILLETS, CUT IN HALF
- KOSHER SALT
- CREOLE SEASONING
- 2 TABLESPOONS CANOLA OIL
- 1 QUART SHUCKED FRESH LOUISIANA OYSTERS, DRAINED
- 24 MEDIUM GULF SHRIMP, SHELLED AND DEVEINED

SEASON THE CRABS and fish fillets with salt and Creole seasoning. Heat the canola oil in a heavy-bottomed skillet over high heat. Add the crabs and cook them until lightly browned. Transfer the crabs to the pot of simmering sauce. Reheat the oil over high heat again and sear the fish fillets until well-browned on the outside but still rare in the center. Transfer the fish to the pot of the simmering sauce. Repeat again with the shrimp. Let the mixture cook together for another ten minutes and then add the oysters to the pot. Continue to simmer until the oysters curl, about two minutes.

TO FINISH THE DISH:
- 6 CUPS WARM WHITE RICE, COOKED AS PER PACKAGE INSTRUCTIONS
- 1 CUP THINLY SLICED GREEN ONIONS

SERVE the court bouillon over rice and top with green onions.

CHRIS HASTINGS

FISHERMEN: Chris Hastings | Zeb Hastings

FISHING GUIDE: Graham Tayloe

FROM THE TIME I was a very young boy, I was a fisherman. It came to me instinctively, providing endless hours on all types of water and instilling in me a deep and abiding love for the restorative power of water. Movement, sound, power, and the array of ecosystems I discovered were nothing short of magical, sacred places for me.

LAKE MARTIN, AL

CHRIS HASTINGS
BIRMINGHAM, AL

Hastings is the executive chef at the award-winning Hot and Hot Fish Club and OvenBird, which he owns with his wife Idie. At OvenBird, a live-fire restaurant, the food is inspired by open-fire cooking from the regions of Spain, Uruguay, Argentina, Portugal, and the American South. Hastings was twice a finalist for the James Beard Best Chef South Award, which he won in 2012. He competed in Food Network's *Iron Chef America* and triumphed over Chef Bobby Flay, 2012, and appeared on *Bizarre Foods America*, 2013. He is author of *The Hot and Hot Fish Club Cookbook, A Celebration of Food, Family, and Traditions* (Running Press, 2009).

I ALSO LEARNED that if you physically, intellectually, and emotionally avail yourself of the waters you fish, eventually you develop a compelling connection and relationship with the earth and its rhythms. You learn to read water, understand the life cycles within it, feel when the bite is on or off, understand its movement and how that movement affects the life within. By deepening that relationship with the earth and the water you become a fisherman.

Fishing and that intimate relationship with water have provided many hours of reflective solitude in both the happiest and most dire times in my life. It has been and always will be Big Medicine for me.

By the time I was 12 I had saved up enough money from my paper route to buy my first fly rod. It was an ugly blue fiberglass piece of crap but I loved it and learned to fly fish with it. By 14 I had caught my first wild trout on the Lineville River in North Carolina on a fly I had tied myself, a royal wolf. It was a 6-inch native brown trout, to this day the most important fish I have ever caught.

Fast forward 25 years. My wife and I are the parents of two boys, Zeb and Vince, who were at that time 3 and 5 years old. As you might imagine, providing my boys the opportunity to develop, at a very young age, a similar window into the hope and magic that is fishing and the outdoors was incredibly important to me. As it turned out, some of our dearest friends in Birmingham had a 3,000-acre property with three lakes just 25 minutes from our front door.

The "Belcher property" is truly a paradise. We spent untold number of hours learning to fish together while discovering nature and life's rhythm found there. Belcher was where we caught hundreds of fish, identified the tracks of and found wild turkeys, bobcats, raccoons, coyotes, otters, and deer. We caught water snakes with our hands and cruised the shorelines on hot summer days in a jon boat looking for water moccasins. Zeb and Vince often recall the day we came across a massive timber rattlesnake, the sight and sound of which we will never forget. We were always wandering the woods after fishing and one day found a small spring fed watering hole deep in the woods; it was crystal clear and icy cold. On hot summer days we would strip down to our birthday suits and take a much-needed swim after fishing all day. It is to this day a magical place for my boys and me. I call it the fountain of youth.

Those were formative years for our boys. Instead of opening more restaurants, we lived a simpler life together, not missing opportunities to suck the marrow out of life's bones. That we did. Best decision we ever made.

For those of you with children, what we know is that they are each unique in the world and have their own very different personalities. While both boys love to fish, Zeb our older son and I developed a profound and, to this day, a real love of fly fishing together. Vincent never learned nor cared to learn to fly fish. Vince is my turkey hunter, but that is another story for another day.

"Movement, sound, power, and the array of ecosystems I discovered were nothing short of magical, sacred places for me."

Belcher is where I taught Zeb how to fly fish. Much like a world-class bird dog puppy that you are training, I quickly realized that he had a natural instinct and would require very little training. Your job as trainer is to teach a puppy the basic yard commands and not to over-handle him. That's all I needed to do with Zeb. He had the nose for it.

From the day I put a fly rod in Zeb's hand or put him on any body of water, I could see and feel that he understood the hope of it. If you fly fish you understand the simple beauty, the feel of fly casting and having the perfect instrument in your hand to connect you to the water and the hope. He is a beautiful fly caster and the fly rod became an extension of him almost immediately. I love to watch him fish.

From that day 20 years ago until today Zeb and I have fished all over the world. While we have caught a lot of fish, the catch has never really defined success or hope. Success for us was being there together. It has been our thing, an unspoken place of quiet joy, a profound love of just being on the water together. The hope, of course, is that we give ourselves up to the water and let a deeper connection to all things be possible through it.

By definition, the Holy Grail is a dish, a plate, a stone, or cup that has special powers and is designed to provide happiness, eternal youth, and food in infinite abundance. It is the salver to the feast. As parents, we are always looking for the "Holy Grail" for our children. For Zeb and me, fly-fishing is that plate.

If the fly rod is the plate, the salver to the feast, the "food" we consume in abundance is the slowing down that allows us to connect intellectually and emotionally to the water and to each other in a real way. The mindful stillness is a deliberate act. It's a choice we make and we are truly nourished by it.

Fly fishing requires a rhythm, the earth's rhythm, our rhythm. The pace nourishes our profound unspoken love of our safe place, where no matter what is going on in our overly busy lives, Zeb and I will find time to fish together. Zeb has never expressed this to me, but I know it happens when we are together fly fishing.

This is the "Holy Grail" for me as a father. A truly holy place that possesses special powers, designed to provide happiness, eternal youth, and food of infinite abundance.

Zeb called me last week. He wants to fish Hatchet Creek, a beautiful stream in Alabama. It is a two-day float with overnight camping on a shoal eating what we catch over a campfire and sleeping under a billion stars. Just the two of us. ✿

"The pace nourishes our profound unspoken love of our safe place, where no matter what is going on in our overly busy lives, Zeb and I will find time to fish together."

THE GUIDE

GRAHAM TAYLOE

WITH **CHRIS HASTINGS**

FISHING HAS BEEN Graham Tayloe's obsession for as long as he can remember. He was 17 when he took his father's friend on his first paid guided fishing trip, a day that would forever change his life. "When we got back to the truck that day the man asked for another guided trip. Seeing that joy and excitement in somebody put a smile on my face for weeks. After 18 years of guiding, I have come to realize the smiles and excitement I see in other people when they catch a fish is what keeps me going."

THE STRIPED BASS is the ultimate predator of freshwater: No fish is safe around them. Their number one prey in our Alabama rivers is gizzard shad, but any fish under a foot in length is fair game. Stripers have a strong ability to analyze not just your bait but also the angler. If you blow into the river making a lot noise, the fish will not leave the area but they know you are there and won't bite a thing.

With stripers, the simpler and stealthier your presentation, whether it be a live bait or a fly, is key. When fishing live bait, I like a 20-30 pound fluorocarbon leader with a tiny No.1 hook. A striper is not going to swim up and crash your bait, it is going to swim up and analyze your bait and if everything is perfect then he will eat it. Same goes for catching big stripes on a fly. The best fly hands-down is a single feather fly with little to no action; the fancier your fly looks the faster the fish will refuse it. The best feathers are from herons and egrets. I just find feathers floating in the river and tie a hook to them.

All the stripers I fish for are land-locked striped bass stocked by the state at 3 per acre. I release 100 percent of my striped bass catch, and I ask all my clients to do the same.

DAVE'S SUMMER SALAD

SERVES 4

This salad was born out of availability. Almost all of the ingredients are grown by farmer Dave Garfrerick during the summer months. Feel free to substitute other produce if some of the ingredients are not available in your area. If good quality eggplant is hard to find, but beautiful baby squash are plentiful, use them instead. I believe that cooking is dependent upon great ingredients. It's an art, not a science. Have fun, be flexible, and allow the quality of the product to rule your purchasing decisions.

- 1 LARGE HEIRLOOM TOMATO, SLICED INTO 8 ROUNDS (½-INCH THICK)
- ¼ CUP BALSAMIC VINEGAR
- 2 TABLESPOONS CHOPPED FRESH BASIL
- 2 TABLESPOONS CHOPPED GREEN ONIONS
- 8 EGGPLANT SLICES (¾-INCH THICK)
- 1 ¼ TEASPOONS KOSHER SALT
- ½ TEASPOON FRESHLY GROUND BLACK PEPPER
- 2 SMALL HEIRLOOM PEPPERS, SUCH AS ANAHEIM, CUBANO, BANANA, OR POBLANO PEPPERS, ROASTED, SEEDED AND PEELED
- 2 TABLESPOONS EXTRA-VIRGIN OLIVE OIL
- ½ CUP FRESH GOAT CHEESE
- ½ CUP BASIL PESTO
- ¼ CUP FRESH MICROGREENS, FOR GARNISH

ARRANGE THE TOMATOES in a 7 x 11-inch baking dish. Pour the vinegar over the tomatoes and add the basil and green onions. Allow the tomatoes to marinate at room temperature for at least 20 minutes.

While the tomatoes are marinating, preheat the grill to medium-high heat (350°F to 400°F).

Season the eggplant slices with salt and pepper and set aside for 10 minutes. Cut the roasted peppers into 8 equal-sized squares and set aside until ready to serve.

Lightly brush the eggplant slices on both sides with the olive oil. Grill the eggplant slices for 2 minutes on each side, or until lightly browned and softened. Remove the slices from the grill and top each slice with 1 tablespoon of the goat cheese. Spoon 1 tablespoon of the pesto on each of 4 salad plates. Place a goat cheese topped eggplant slice on each plate. Arrange a roasted pepper square over each eggplant and top each pepper with a tomato slice. Repeat layers with the remaining eggplant, pepper, and tomato slices, until all of the vegetables have been used. Drizzle 1 tablespoon of the remaining pesto around each vegetable stack. Arrange 1 tablespoon of microgreens on top of each salad. Serve immediately.

Recipe from *Hot & Hot Fish Club cookbook* (Running Press Book Publishers, 2009)

GRILLED NY STRIP WITH POACHED FARM EGG, PARMIGIANO-REGGIANO, AND TRUFFLE OIL

SERVES 6

Everyone has a favorite cut of steak to eat, but the addition of the poached farm egg takes this entrée into the realm of "breakfast" or a great "late night" dinner. The sharpness of the Parmigiano-Reggiano and the scent of the truffle oil sets this plate apart from the regular steak entrée. If you don't like one of the three components (egg, cheese, or truffle oil) you can still make this dish with your favorite component.

- 24 FINGERLING POTATOES
- 2 (8-OUNCE) BUNCHES FRESH RAPINI OR BROCCOLI RABE
- ¼ CUP PLUS 2 TABLESPOONS EXTRA-VIRGIN OLIVE OIL
- 2 LARGE GARLIC CLOVES, PEELED
- 1 TEASPOON CRUSHED RED PEPPER
- 6 NEW YORK STRIP STEAKS (16-OUNCE EACH)
- 2 TABLESPOONS HASTINGS CREATIONS ALL-PURPOSE HERB SALT OR KOSHER SALT
- 2 TABLESPOONS PLUS ¼ TEASPOON FRESHLY GROUND BLACK PEPPER, DIVIDED
- 1 TEASPOON KOSHER SALT
- 6 LARGE POACHED EGGS
- 1½ CUPS FRESHLY GRATED PARMIGIANO-REGGIANO CHEESE
- 2 TABLESPOONS BLACK TRUFFLE OIL

Recipe from *Hot & Hot Fish Club cookbook* (Running Press Book Publishers, 2009)

PREHEAT THE GRILL to medium-high heat (350°F to 400°F)

Place the potatoes in a medium saucepan with a small handful of salt. Add enough cold water to cover the potatoes and bring to a boil over high heat. Reduce the heat to medium-low and simmer for 8 to 10 minutes or just until tender. Drain and set aside to cool completely, about 30 minutes. Cut the potatoes in half lengthwise.

Bring a medium saucepan of salted water to a boil over medium-high heat. Add the rapini and cook until bright green and tender, about 2 minutes. Drain the rapini and rinse under cold running water. Set aside.

Heat the olive oil in a small skillet over medium heat. Add the garlic and crushed red pepper and cook until the garlic begins to brown, 1 to 2 minutes. Remove from the heat and set aside to cool slightly.

Preheat the oven to 400°F.

Season the steaks evenly on both sides with the herb salt and 2 tablespoons of the pepper, using about 1 teaspoon of the salt and 1 teaspoon of the pepper on each steak. Grill the steaks over medium-high heat for 5 to 6 minutes on the first side, turn and continue cooking for 3 to 4 minutes (for medium) or until desired degree of doneness.

Transfer steaks to a warm platter and loosely cover with aluminum foil for at least 5 minutes before serving.

Combine the olive oil and garlic mixture, potatoes, rapini, 1 teaspoon of the salt and ¼ teaspoon of the pepper in a large bowl and toss until well coated. Pour the vegetable mixture into a large baking dish and bake at 400°F for 10 minutes or until heated through.

Divide the rapini and potato mixture evenly between 6 dinner plates. Arrange 1 steak on each serving of vegetables and top with a poached egg. Sprinkle ¼ cup of the Parmesan over each serving and drizzle with 1 teaspoon each of truffle oil. Serve immediately.

WILD TURKEY SALAD WITH FIRST OF THE SEASON MORELS AND WATERCRESS

SERVES 4

Opening day of turkey hunting season in Alabama is one of the most anticipated days on our calendar. I'm sharing this favorite recipe for wild turkey in the hope that doing so will bring us luck in harvesting a prized gobbler next season. If you don't have a good shot at a wild turkey this year, substitute fresh, domestic turkey breast. Partially freezing the turkey breast makes for easier slicing. Happy Hunting and Eating!

FOR THE TURKEY:
- ¼ CUP BUTTERMILK
- 1 TABLESPOON DIJON MUSTARD
- 1½ TEASPOONS KOSHER SALT, DIVIDED
- 1 TEASPOON FRESHLY GROUND BLACK PEPPER, DIVIDED
- 12 SLICES (1/8-INCH THICK) WILD TURKEY BREAST, ABOUT 4 TO 5 OUNCES
- 3 CUPS FRESH BREADCRUMBS
- ¼ CUP PEANUT OIL, FOR COOKING

COMBINE THE BUTTERMILK and the mustard with 1/2 teaspoon of the salt and 1/2 teaspoon pepper in a shallow dish. Add the turkey slices, turning to coat. Cover and allow the turkey to marinate in the refrigerator for 1 hour.

Season the breadcrumbs with the remaining teaspoon of salt and 1/2 teaspoon of pepper. Dredge the turkey slices in the breadcrumbs, pressing to make sure the crumbs adhere to the turkey. Place the breaded turkey on a parchment paper-lined plate. (At this point the turkey can be covered and refrigerated up to 2 hours, if needed.)

Just before serving, heat the peanut oil in a large cast-iron skillet over medium-high heat until hot. Add the turkey, in batches as to not overcrowd the skillet, and cook 11/2 to 2 minutes on each side or until golden brown. Transfer to a paper towel-lined plate to drain. Repeat with the remaining turkey slices. Cover to keep warm.

FOR THE LEMON-DIJON VINAIGRETTE:
- ½ CUP PLUS 2 TABLESPOONS FRESHLY SQUEEZED LEMON JUICE
- ¼ CUP DIJON MUSTARD
- ½ CUP OLIVE OIL
- ½ CUP EXTRA-VIRGIN OLIVE OIL
- 2 TABLESPOONS FINELY CHOPPED SHALLOTS
- 2 TABLESPOONS FINELY CHOPPED FRESH PARSLEY
- ½ TEASPOON FINELY CHOPPED FRESH THYME
- ½ TEASPOON KOSHER SALT
- ½ TEASPOON FRESHLY GROUND BLACK PEPPER

IN A BOWL, whisk together the lemon juice, mustard, and olive oils. Stir in the shallots, parsley, and thyme. Season with salt and pepper. Refrigerate until ready to serve.

FOR THE SALAD:
- 1 TABLESPOON OLIVE OIL
- 1 TABLESPOON MINCED SHALLOTS
- ¼ TEASPOON CHOPPED FRESH THYME
- 3 OUNCES FRESH MOREL MUSHROOMS
- PINCH OF KOSHER SALT
- PINCH OF FRESHLY GROUND BLACK PEPPER
- 12 CUPS (1½ BUNCHES) LOOSELY PACKED FRESH WATERCRESS
- 2 OUNCES FRESH CHÈVRE GOAT CHEESE, CRUMBLED
- 2 TABLESPOONS FINELY CHOPPED FRESH CHIVES

HEAT THE OLIVE oil in a small skillet over medium-high heat. Add the shallots, thyme, and mushrooms and cook until softened, 4 to 5 minutes. Season the mushrooms with a pinch each of salt and pepper and remove from the heat. Allow mushrooms to cool for 10 minutes before tossing the salad.

Combine the watercress and the cooled mushrooms in a large bowl with about 1/4 cup of the vinaigrette, toss until well coated. Layer one-third of the watercress mixture on each of 4 serving plates. Top each salad with 1 slice of fried turkey. Repeat the layers two more times. Crumble about 1/2 ounce of the goat cheese and 1/2 tablespoon of the chives over each salad and serve immediately.

Recipe from *Hot & Hot Fish Club* cookbook (Running Press Book Publishers, 2009)

FIRST-OF-THE-SEASON STRAWBERRY SHORTCAKES WITH HONEYSUCKLE CRÈME FRAÎCHE

SERVES 8

As a child, my family would go out each May and pick strawberries from the local "pick your own" farms around Charlotte, North Carolina where we lived. My mother was a great cook and she loved the adventure of foraging for food as much as she did cooking. The smell and taste of a perfectly ripe strawberry that is still warm from the sun is one of my favorite childhood food memories. Sadly, juicy ripe strawberries are hard to find these days. Look for fresh strawberries at your local farmers' market that are red all the way through and that are naturally sweet with a slight tanginess. You can use this shortcake recipe throughout the summer, switching out the strawberries for whatever berry is in season.

Recipe from *Hot & Hot Fish Club cookbook* (Running Press Book Publishers, 2009)

FOR THE HONEYSUCKLE SYRUP:
- 2 CUPS GRANULATED SUGAR
- 1 CUP WATER
- 3 OUNCES FRESH GOLDEN-YELLOW HONEYSUCKLE BLOSSOMS

COMBINE THE SUGAR and water in a small saucepan and bring to a boil, stirring occasionally until the sugar is dissolved. Boil for 30 seconds and remove the saucepan from the heat.

Pack a 1-quart Mason jar with a tight-fitting lid with the honeysuckle blossoms. Pour the hot simple syrup over the fresh blossoms and allow the mixture to cool to room temperature. Once cool enough to touch, seal the jar and chill overnight.

The honeysuckle syrup will keep in the refrigerator for up to one week. Both the syrup and the honeysuckle blossoms can be used in recipes.

FOR THE HONEYSUCKLE CRÈME FRAÎCHE:
- 1 ¾ CUPS CRÈME FRAÎCHE
- 2 TABLESPOONS HONEYSUCKLE SIMPLE SYRUP
- 1 TABLESPOON FINELY CHOPPED HONEYSUCKLE BLOSSOMS

WHISK TOGETHER the crème fraîche and simple syrup until the mixture begins to stiffen and forms medium-soft peaks. Fold in the honeysuckle blossoms.

Refrigerate for 4 hours to allow the flavors of the honeysuckle to intensify.

FOR THE STRAWBERRIES:
- 1 CONTAINER (16-OUNCE) FRESH STRAWBERRIES, HULLED AND QUARTERED (ABOUT 2 ½ CUPS)
- 3 TABLESPOONS GRANULATED SUGAR
- 2 TABLESPOONS FRESHLY SQUEEZED LEMON JUICE

COMBINE THE STRAWBERRIES, sugar, and lemon juice in a small glass or stainless steel bowl. Cover and chill for at least 30 minutes, stirring occasionally.

FOR THE SHORTCAKES:
- 2 CUPS ALL-PURPOSE FLOUR, PLUS MORE FOR ROLLING OUT THE DOUGH
- 1 TEASPOON BAKING POWDER
- ½ TEASPOON SALT
- 1 TABLESPOON GRANULATED SUGAR
- ½ CUP (1 STICK) CHILLED UNSALTED BUTTER, DICED
- ¾ CUP PLUS 1 TABLESPOON WHOLE-MILK BUTTERMILK, DIVIDED
- 1 TABLESPOON COARSE, RAW SUGAR
- 1½ CUPS HONEYSUCKLE CRÈME FRAÎCHE

MIX TOGETHER 2 cups of the flour, the baking powder, salt, and sugar in a large bowl. Cut the butter into the flour mixture until pea-sized pieces are formed. Refrigerate the flour and butter mixture, until well chilled, about 30 minutes.

Slowly add 3/4 cup of the buttermilk into the chilled flour mixture and blend until a dough begins to come together. Be careful not to over-mix or the shortcakes will be tough.

Preheat the oven to 425°F.

Place the dough onto a lightly floured work surface and pat down into a 1-inch thick circle. Using a 1 1/2-inch round cutter, cut as many shortcakes as you can out of the dough. Gently pull together the dough scraps and pat into a 1-inch thick circle. Continue cutting out shortcakes with the remaining dough.

Place the shortcakes onto an ungreased baking sheet and brush the tops with the remaining tablespoon of buttermilk. Sprinkle the coarse sugar evenly over the tops of the shortcakes. Bake for 13 to 15 minutes or until golden brown, remove from the oven, and cool slightly.

Cut the shortcakes in half, horizontally, and place 2 halves on each of the 8 dessert plates. Spoon 1/4 cup of the macerated strawberries and their juices onto the bottom half of each shortcake. Place 2 to 3 tablespoons of the crème fraîche over each of the strawberries and top each with the top half of the shortcake. Serve immediately.

DONALD LINK

FISHERMEN: Donald Link | Gene Link | Nico Link

TOLEDO BEND
RESERVOIR, LA

I'M NOT SURE WHICH MEMORY sticks out in my mind first, the first time I caught a fish or the first time I cleaned a fish. They were on the same day and it seems like yesterday. ¶ Like many who grew up fishing, I have a romanticized memory of my early days on the water and my eagerness to get after the next catch.

DONALD LINK
NEW ORLEANS, LA

Link's restaurant Herbsaint earned him a James Beard Foundation Award, Best Chef South, 2007. That same year Cochon was nominated Best New Restaurant and Link's cookbook, *Real Cajun: Rustic Home Cooking from Donald Link's Louisiana* (Clarkson Potter) won Best American Cookbook. Link was also nominated by the James Beard Foundation for the prestigious award of Outstanding Chef in 2012, 2013, 2014, and 2016, and Pêche Seafood Grill was awarded Best New Restaurant in 2014.

I CAN READILY RECALL the anticipation and excitement of the pole bowing down and reeling in the beautifully colored specimens of different types of fish, from the deep brown-and-gold bream to the silvery, spotted, green-hued perch.

Toledo Bend Lake, the renowned bass fishery on the Louisiana-Texas border, is where I spent most of my early days learning to fish. Naturally bass is the main prize, yet for me there is the mysterious if not somewhat scary catfish. Scary because of the constant warnings of how they will sting or "fin" you if you hold them the wrong way. Scary also because Grandad would bring in catfish as large as me from the trotlines he had set around the lake. Nonetheless, the catfish was and always will be my favorite from these waters.

Oddly enough, the fish that is the most fun to catch, the bass, was always my least favorite to eat. In this chapter you'll see a recipe for how my Grandad cooked his fish. I still use his method to this day, at Toledo Bend for sure. Scaled, gutted, beheaded, dragged in cornmeal, and fried in an iron skillet. The only way.

My Grandad stands out in my mind as a legend, a spiritual, almost mythical, entity who was part of that lake and still is. That man caught fish every time we went on the water. He was one with that lake. I remember slowly floating on the boat through a minefield of stumps and submerged trees sticking up out of the water, which he would navigate with ease to get to his spots, where we would pull fish out at will. One night under the bridge we pulled perch out of the water faster than I thought humanly possible. He taught me how to tie knots, how to cast, what bait to use, you name it. Combine all that with the garden of fresh okra, eggplant, peaches, tomatoes, black-eyed peas, and green beans. Not only was the fishing memorable, but we also had some of the best meals of my life at Toledo Bend Lake.

Today our tradition carries on with my daughter and son learning from my father. All the magic I felt being at the lake is alive and well inside them. I see myself in them, whether we are fishing at sunrise or just watching the sunset from the boat. I have taken my Grandad's place as cook, which I may actually enjoy now more than the fishing. We have new traditions now as well. Late-night card games and movies on rainy days are a new part of our life at Toledo, not to mention lots of drinking and good times.

Food and cooking were always a huge part of the camp. Breakfast always starts when I get back from the morning bass run. Normally it includes bacon, grits, and biscuits, but depending on the night before it could be a crawfish-egg casserole with cheddar, or a chicken hash made from last night's grilled chicken. Each trip will always have one thing for sure and that's fried fish. The sides are the main items that will change around, so I've added a couple here in the recipe section.

I've been fishing and shrimping almost everywhere I can think of in Louisiana. The marshlands south of New Orleans have some of the best fishing I've seen. Redfish tops the list of my favorite fish, but those you don't fry, you grill them.

I've been offshore in Florida for American redfish and cobia, salmon fishing in Alaska, and trout fishing in Arkansas and Wyoming, but Toledo Bend is more than the fishing for me. It's actually where I catch the least fish, but that's not what it's about.

It's the flock of geese flying low over the lake at dawn while the steam rising from the water creates a layer of mist. It's the grace of the blue herons, and the silvery wake of clear water the boat creates as we head out.

Mostly, though, it's sitting on the boat drinking a beer while the night sky takes over the sunset as we prepare for the next round of night fishing. ✺

"Today our tradition carries on with my daughter and son learning from my father. All the magic I felt being at the lake is alive and well inside them. I see myself in them, whether we are fishing at sunrise or just watching the sunset from the boat."

"In this chapter you'll see a recipe for how my Grandad cooked his fish. I still use his method to this day at Toledo Bend for sure. Scaled, gutted, beheaded, dragged in cornmeal, and fried in an iron skillet. The only way."

FRIED BASS

SERVES 6

I grew up eating these white cornmeal-encrusted bass with my Grandad. I guess you could use yellow cornmeal, but I prefer white cornmeal because that's what my Grandad used.

Frying smaller fresh-caught lake fish like bass, perch, and bluegills whole rather than filleted is the way to go. There is just so much flavor in the skin and fins – and this is especially true with the fish we catch here in Toledo Bend.

Cooking Tip: *You want the fish pieces to be about the size of your hand. Depending on the size, I usually cut the bass in half or possibly thirds. Smaller fish like perch and bluegills, I leave whole.*

- 6 BASS (ABOUT 1 ½ POUNDS EACH), SCALED AND GUTTED
- 1 CUP WHITE CORNMEAL
- 1 CUP ALL-PURPOSE FLOUR
- KOSHER SALT AND FRESHLY GROUND BLACK PEPPER
- VEGETABLE OIL, FOR FRYING

REMOVE THE HEADS and cut each bass in half crosswise.

Place the cornmeal and flour in a shallow bowl and whisk to combine. Generously season the fish with salt and pepper.

Dredge the fish through the cornmeal mixture, evenly coating on all sides. Place the prepared fish on a baking sheet or cutting board.

In a large stockpot or cast-iron Dutch oven, pour enough oil so that there is approximately a 3 to 4-inch layer of oil. Over medium-high heat, warm the oil until it reaches 350°F. In batches so as not to over crowd the pot, cook the fish, turning half way though with a slotted spoon to cook on all sides, until golden brown and cooked through, about 5 to 8 minutes depending on the size of the fish. Transfer to a paper towel-lined plate to drain and season with more salt and pepper to taste. Repeat with the remaining fish.

Serve immediately.

DONALD'S POTATO SALAD

SERVES 6 TO 8

This is not your ordinary potato salad.

This salad was inspired by a trip to South America. The versions of potato salad I enjoyed down in Uruguay had a fresh brightness to them thanks to the addition of cilantro and the use of vinaigrette as the dressing. I have been opting for this mayonnaise-free style of potato salad ever since that trip.

As I developed my favorite version of this salad, I found that I preferred to use prosciutto rather than bacon. Unlike bacon, prosciutto is not smoked ... thus offering a brighter flavor to a dish.

FOR THE SALAD:
- 3 CUPS PEELED AND DICED SWEET POTATOES, CUT INTO 1-INCH PIECES
- 3 CUPS DICED YUKON GOLD POTATOES, CUT INTO 1-INCH PIECES
- 1 TEASPOON OLIVE OIL
- 4 OUNCES PROSCIUTTO, CUT INTO 1-INCH PIECES
- ½ RED ONION, THINLY SLICED
- ½ CUP ROUGH-CHOPPED FRESH CILANTRO

PUT THE POTATOES in a large heavy-bottomed pot and cover with water by 2 inches. Bring to a boil over high heat. Reduce the heat to medium-low and simmer just until they are tender but still firm, about 15 to 20 minutes. Drain and set aside to cool completely.

While the potatoes are cooking, heat the oil in a pan over medium-high heat. Add the prosciutto and cook until crispy. Transfer to a paper towel-lined plate to drain.

FOR THE VINAIGRETTE:
- 2 TABLESPOONS RED WINE VINEGAR
- 2 TABLESPOONS WHOLE-GRAIN MUSTARD
- ½ CUP OLIVE OIL
- KOSHER SALT AND FRESHLY GROUND BLACK PEPPER

WHISK TOGETHER the vinegar and mustard. Slowly whisk in the olive oil until emulsified. Season with salt and pepper to taste.

Place the potatoes in a large serving bowl. Add the prosciutto, red onion, and cilantro and toss to combine. Add the vinaigrette to taste and toss to coat. Taste for seasonings, adding more salt and pepper as desired.

Cover and refrigerate until ready to serve. Serve chilled.

CRUSTY CORNBREAD

SERVES 6 TO 8

This recipe belongs to my Grandad. He made it for me when I was a kid ... and now I use the same recipe when cooking for my family at Toledo Bend.

What makes this cornbread special is it's dense and crusty texture. It's held its shape under smothered greens, stewed beans, ... basically anything with a fragrant broth, while softer-crumbed versions fell apart.

For the best and crispiest results, pour the batter into a hot cast-iron skillet. In a pinch you can use a baking pan, but cast-iron always creates the best crust (and looks great on the table).

I always run a stick of butter over the hot cornbread when it comes out of the oven (allowing about 2 tablespoons of it to melt) for added flavor.

- 2 CUPS ALL-PURPOSE FLOUR
- 2 CUPS WHITE CORNMEAL
- 2 TABLESPOONS SUGAR
- 2 TEASPOONS BAKING POWDER
- 1 TABLESPOON KOSHER SALT
- 1/2 TEASPOON FRESHLY GROUND BLACK PEPPER
- 1 CUP WELL-SHAKEN BUTTERMILK
- 1 1/2 CUPS MILK
- 1 LARGE EGG
- 6 TABLESPOONS BUTTER, MELTED
- 1 TABLESPOON RENDERED BACON FAT, OR BUTTER, SHORTENING, OR VEGETABLE OIL

PREHEAT THE OVEN to 400°F.

Place a 12-inch cast-iron skillet in the oven and heat for at least 30 minutes. Meanwhile, make the batter.

Whisk together the flour, cornmeal, sugar, baking powder, salt, and pepper in a large bowl. In a separate medium bowl, whisk together the buttermilk, milk, egg, and the 6 tablespoons melted butter.

Make a well in the center of the dry ingredients and pour the wet ingredients into the well. Use a fork or rubber spatula to stir together until evenly combined.

Remove the skillet from oven, add the bacon fat to the skillet, and swirl to coat. Pour the batter into the hot skillet, spread the batter evenly, and bake for 25 to 35 minutes, until lightly golden and firm and springy to the touch. Serve immediately or cool the cornbread in the skillet and serve at room temperature.

LAKE BEANS

SERVES 6 TO 8

White beans have been a staple I have grown up with. To me, they taste better than the red beans that so many folks in Louisiana use.

I like my beans with a bit of a kick. A little jalapeño (or you could use poblano if you prefer) adds heat while the additions of whole-grain mustard and red wine vinegar add a delicious bite to the dish.

Cooking Tip: *I recommend soaking white beans before cooking them. It just makes the whole cooking process go better if you do. If you choose not to soak the beans, you will need to add more water and cook them longer.*

- 1 POUND DRIED WHITE BEANS (ANY VARIETY)
- 1 TABLESPOON BUTTER OR BACON FAT
- 1 POUND BEST-QUALITY SMOKED ANDOUILLE SAUSAGE, CUT IN ½-INCH DICE
- 1 MEDIUM ONION, DICED
- 2 TO 3 CELERY STALKS, DICED
- 4 TO 5 GARLIC CLOVES, MINCED
- 1 JALAPEÑO PEPPER, STEMMED, SEEDED, AND MINCED
- 6 BAY LEAVES
- 2 TEASPOONS KOSHER SALT
- 2 TEASPOONS FRESHLY GROUND BLACK PEPPER
- 1 TABLESPOON CREOLE OR WHOLE-GRAIN MUSTARD
- 2 TABLESPOONS RED WINE VINEGAR
- 12 CUPS (3 QUARTS) WATER
- 2 CUPS FRESH GREEN BEANS, TRIMMED AND CUT

PLACE THE BEANS in a large pot with enough water to cover them by 4 inches. Soak the beans a minimum of 6 hours or up to overnight.

Heat the butter or bacon fat in a heavy-bottomed pot over medium-high heat.

Add the sausage and cook until browned, about 4 to 5 minutes.

Add the onion, celery, garlic, jalapeño, bay leaves, salt, and pepper, and cook, stirring, until the vegetables have softened, about 10 minutes.

Add the mustard and vinegar. Cook for 2 minutes more, stirring occasionally.

Drain and rinse the beans and add them to the pot along with the 12 cups of fresh water.

Bring to a boil, then reduce the heat to low and cook at a simmer for about 30 minutes.

Add the green beans and cook until the beans are tender, for 20 to 30 minutes more. Discard the bay leaves.

Taste for seasonings, adding more salt and pepper as desired.

KEVIN
WILLMANN

FISHERMEN: Kevin Willmann | Jessica Willmann
Rino Taylor | Eric Landis | Frank Taylor
FISHING GUIDE: Victor Wright

PENSACOLA, FL

THE ST. LOUIS winters are hard for me. In the dead of winter, the sun falls before the clock strikes five and the stark emptiness and dormancy of everything green puts me in a funk every year. There's only one prescription: a heavy dose of the Gulf Coast spring and the pursuit of cobia!

KEVIN WILLMANN
ST LOUIS, MO

Willmann, chef and owner of Farmhaus Restaurant with his wife Jessica, was born into a farming family in Greenville, Illinois, and self-taught in the culinary arts in the Florida Panhandle. Multiple-year nominee for James Beard Foundation Awards. Finalist for James Beard Foundation, Best Chef, Midwest, 2016, semifinalist for Best Chef, Midwest, 2015. Won *Food & Wine* Best New Chef in 2011. Participated in *Food & Wine*'s Chef's Club restaurant at the St. Regis in Aspen, Colorado, 2012, and appeared on *Bizarre Foods America*, 2013.

IMMEDIATELY AFTER the hustle of the holidays and the celebration of the New Year, I begin the work of building and repairing the cobia rods. I repair or replace every imaginable piece of equipment, every pump and light bulb on the boat. I take stock of the state of the tools we use to hunt the fish that many of us have elevated to somewhere between a reason to live and life itself.

Reels are meticulously torn down, lubed, and reassembled with a watchmaker's care. I order parts to replace those that are broken, spool all of the reels with thousands of yards of fresh line, double- and triple-check everything. Proven hooks are ordered in bulk, leaders are tied.

From early January until the last week of March this is my second job; prepping my station—my life—for April. I spend the workdays preparing my restaurant crew to run things without me for a few weeks. I spend the late nights after service planning and checking things off the list. Nearly 90 days pass in the blink of an eye and then it's finally here: April.

The migration is on. It's time to pack. It's time to hunt cobia.

Two groups of cobia leave the Caribbean sometime around January. Some head northeast and travel up the coast to spawning grounds on the East Coast. But others head northwest and start a Gulf Coast migration that will find them traveling all the way past the Mississippi Delta to the Texas Gulf Coast. This second group of fish and their migration has been a subject of complete focus for thousands of Gulf Coast anglers for decades. Their intercept along northwest Florida and the Alabama coast usually begins around the last week of March, give or take, and generally lasts five or six weeks. Tournaments go all month in April from Panama City, Florida, to Orange Beach, Alabama, and beyond.

"I spend the workdays preparing my restaurant crew to run things without me for a few weeks. I spend the late nights after service planning and checking things off the list. Nearly 90 days pass in the blink of an eye and then it's finally here: April. The migration is on. It's time to pack. It's time to hunt cobia."

I love to fish. If there is water enough to support even a single fish, I have likely pursued it. I get it from my grandpa Berry, whose influence was great in my youth. He was always tinkering and often fishing, a retired Methodist preacher who found peace with a pre-rigged black-and-white rubber worm tied to the end of his line. When he passed, we packed up his favorite rod and tied on a black-and-white for him to have for his next journey.

For me, the fresh water of my Illinois youth was just the beginning. Around 1990, my immediate family moved to Gulf Breeze, Florida. I was 12 and it took about 12 seconds before I was addicted forever. My parents rented a little house a couple blocks off of a bayou and it was over.

My neighborhood buds taught me enough to get going and within a couple years I was as much a part of a shoreline somewhere as the herons and ospreys. The backwater pursuit of speckled trout, redfish, and flounder prepared me for sight fishing and larger fish. I mowed a pretty good network of lawns in my new town and I took the opportunities my waterfront customers gave me to fish off of their docks and throw the cast net for mullet and baitfish.

I was about 15 when I got the nerve to ask the local tackle shop for a job. Gulf Breeze Bait and Tackle was not hiring at the time, but their sister business, The Fish Peddler, was, so I pedaled over to the Peddler and started my journey. It would be here that I would learn the local commercial fishing business and get a glimpse into the restaurant business.

"I love to fish. If there is water enough to support even a single fish, I have likely pursued it."

"I have spent countless hours in the tower with my chef, mentor, and best friend Frank Taylor. Chef Frank owns and operates The Global Grill in downtown Pensacola. I came up cooking in his kitchens and helped to open the Global Grill nearly 15 years ago, but our friendship goes back to the mid-90s when Frank gave me a job at a busy Pensacola Beach restaurant. Frank shared my passion for being on the water and had just negotiated the acquisition of his grandfather's little skiff and we began pushing all of life's boundaries to fish."

"So imagine this: Three or more of your best buddies are with you on a perch high off the water searching for migrating fish, sharing stories, sippin' on frosties."

I picked up the craft of custom rod-building along the way and eventually took over the rod shop in the back of Gulf Breeze Bait and Tackle, repairing and building custom rods for the local guys, charter boat captains, and walk-in customers. My buddy Victor Wright bought some of my first cobia rods, and he still orders a couple every year for himself and his crew aboard the Vitamin Sea.

I dabbled as a deck hand and commercial fisherman for a couple years and took every opportunity to go offshore and learn. The deeper I became involved the more my love for one fish above all others grew: Cobia, or ling, as we call them.

Cobia grow quickly and to a large size. Females reach over 100 pounds and the average fish we catch during the migration is generally 30-60 pounds.

We hunt for them from elevated towers on boats, staring for hours into our designated section of water until the moment one is spotted, often sunning on the surface headed west to the spawning grounds. We then present a bait or lure to the fish. We travel slowly down the sand bar from a few feet off the beach out to about a mile or so offshore so that the curious cobia will pop up to investigate the boat.

So imagine this: Three or more of your best buddies are with you on a perch high off the water searching for migrating fish, sharing stories, sippin' on frosties. Can you see the potential? OK, now picture the emerald coast and all the sea life that we encounter during our pursuit: dolphins, giant leatherback turtles, manta rays, mako sharks, schools of tarpon, and jack cravelle.

Then, often out of nowhere, a cobia or a pair or more will be right there! Mayhem ensues, the cast is made, and, more often than not, the fish is hooked. The excitement to land a good fish on generally light tackle—dumping line off the reel—is unbeatable. To share the experience with your buds and the teamwork needed to land said fish is gold.

I have spent countless hours in the tower with my chef, mentor, and best friend Frank Taylor. Chef Frank owns and operates The Global Grill in downtown Pensacola. I came up cooking in his kitchens and helped to open the Global Grill nearly 15 years ago, but our friendship goes back to the mid-90s when Frank gave me a job at a busy Pensacola Beach restaurant. Frank shared my passion for being on the water and had just negotiated the acquisition of his grandfather's little skiff and we began pushing all of life's boundaries to fish. We would stay up all night in the fall to fish for giant bull redfish after busy nights at the restaurant or go straight from Saturday service to packing up the boat to chase king mackerel in the bay at the break of dawn.

Now, a couple decades later, you will still find us fishing a little too much, trading stories, sharing techniques and recipes. If it's April, there's a good chance we're in the tower hunting cobia. ⚙

"The excitement to land a good fish on generally light tackle—dumping line off the reel—is unbeatable. To share the experience with your buds and the teamwork needed to land said fish is gold."

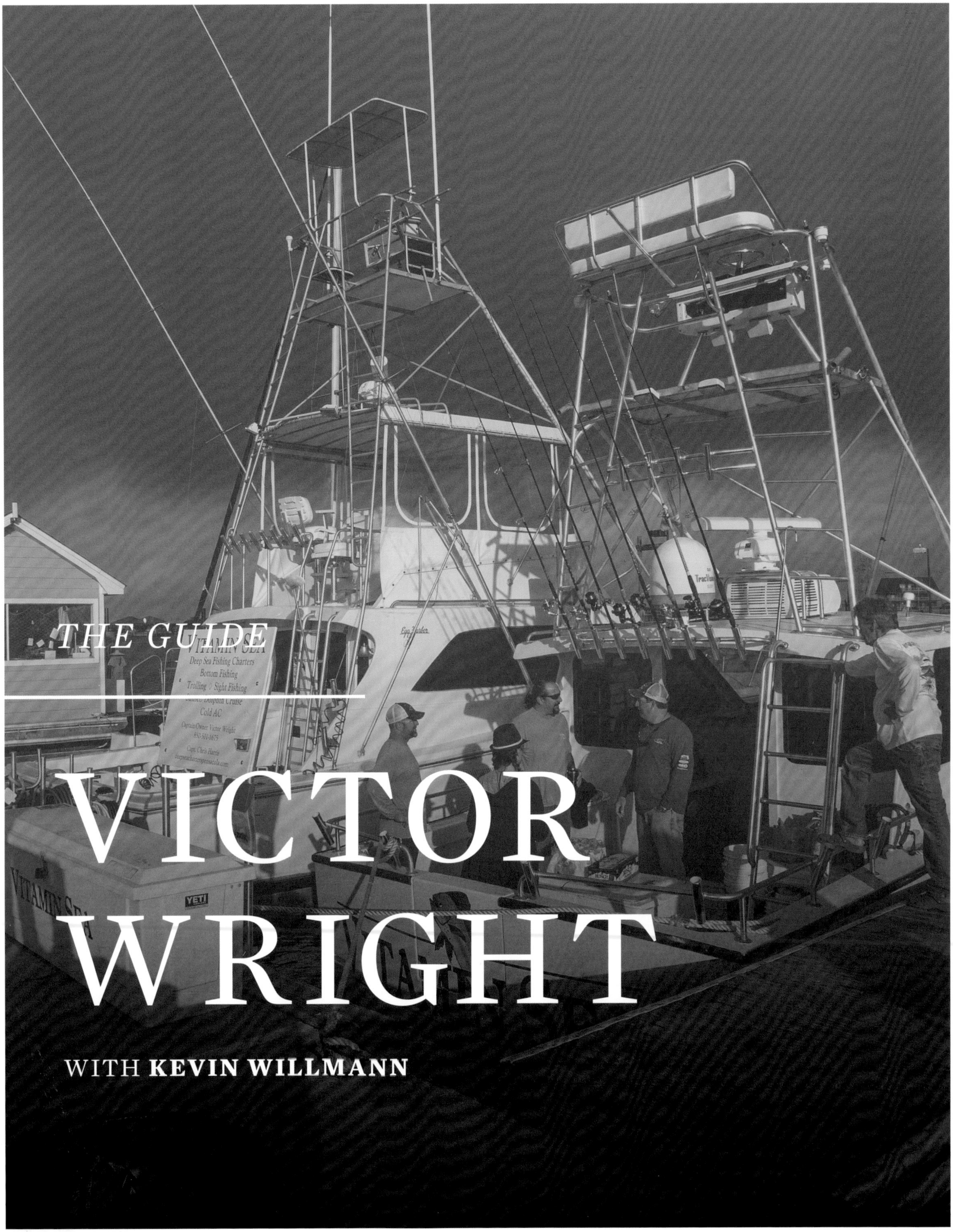

THE GUIDE

VICTOR WRIGHT

WITH **KEVIN WILLMANN**

CAPTAIN VICTOR WRIGHT grew up in a deep-sea fishing family. He and his father John Wright own Gulf Breeze Bait and Tackle and have been in the saltwater tackle business in Pensacola since 1981. Wright, a Gulf Breeze native, has been in the charter fishing business since 1991 and has spent decades mastering his skills and learning what it takes to catch fish. Through hard work and dedication during his early years spent commercial fishing for tuna and red snapper, Captain Victor earned his reputation in the fishing industry. He captains the Vitamin Sea out of Pensacola.

I HAVE BEEN FISHING for cobia for over 30 years. We run cobia charters and also fish several major cobia tournaments every year. The cobia migration in the Florida Panhandle along the white sand beaches runs from about March 15 through May 15. They migrate east to west from the Florida Keys to the nutrient-rich waters of the Mississippi River in Louisiana and also north from the Florida Keys up the east coast of Florida toward North Carolina and Virginia.

Cobia grow to over 100 pounds; the record in Florida is 130.1 pounds. They are caught sight-fishing using live eels, bucktail jigs, and live fish. Spinning reels with 9-foot rods are preferred. Boats with tall towers fish at slow speed looking for cobia ascending and descending in the water column as they migrate. Cobia may be alone or in groups and like to swim under turtles and rays. Cobia fishing is hours of waiting and patience, followed by minutes of pure adrenalin and excitement. The limit is one per person in Florida, so please tag and release all fish you don't want to keep.

CHAR-GRILLED COBIA WITH STEWED TOMATOES AND OKRA

SERVES 6

After a long day out on the water, this recipe is the perfect dish to serve a boatful of hungry cobia fishermen. It's simple ... but sure is delicious.

Cobia is best when it is just barely done. It will be very moist and stark white, and will break apart cleanly between the muscle "flakes." When cooking them, I usually make one or two extra to use as a sacrificial taster piece to check the inside of the fillets for doneness.

Also, thinner cuts of the Cobia are best for quick cooking and retain moisture better than thicker cuts. I cut mine only about 3/4 –inch thick on the bias and cook them really quickly over a super hot fire. (And I mean hot! I try to get my Egg up to about 700°F.) Anything thicker than 3/4-inch tends to dry out before the center is done.

And you may want to start seasoning more Cobia when you pull the first batch off the grill ... everyone will want another piece!

- 6 TABLESPOONS QUALITY OLIVE OIL, DIVIDED
- 1 POUND FRESH OKRA, STEM END REMOVED AND SLICED LONGWISE AND CROSSWISE TO VARY THE TEXTURE
- 3 GARLIC CLOVES, MINCED
- 2 POUNDS RIPE TOMATOES (FRESH FROM THE GARDEN), CUT INTO LARGE WEDGES
- KOSHER SALT AND FRESHLY GROUND BLACK PEPPER
- 1 FRESH BAY LEAF
- CAYENNE PEPPER
- FRESHLY GRATED LEMON ZEST
- 6 COBIA FILLETS, CUT ON THE BIAS ABOUT ¾ INCH THICK

FIRE UP an Egg or a kettle grill with lump charcoal and build a nice big hot fire.

Heat 2 to 3 tablespoons of olive oil in a large sauté pan or a cast iron skillet over medium-high heat. Add the okra and brown slightly, trying to brown the "inside" faces of the okra cut lengthwise as well.

Add the garlic and continue to cook until the garlic is just starting to brown. Add the tomatoes and move them around to deglaze the garlic from the pan. Add a teaspoon or two of Kosher salt, a pinch of black pepper, the bay leaf, and a pinch or two of the cayenne. Lower the heat and simmer gently until the tomatoes give up their juices, about 5 minutes.

Meanwhile, lightly brush the Cobia fillets with the remaining oil. Then season the fish to taste with salt and pepper, lemon zest, and a pinch of cayenne.

Grill the fillets for a couple minutes on the first side, turning once to make some nice grill marks, and then finish on the other side, about 4 to 6 minutes total.

Allow the fillets to rest for just a minute while checking the seasoning on the tomatoes and okra. To serve, spoon the tomato-okra mixture onto a plate and top with a Cobia fillet.

CORN AND SHRIMP SALAD WITH TASSO

SERVES 6

Down in Pensacola, Cobia season coincides with Florida Hopper season. We have gotten to be good friends with a shrimper named Paul Baker and every spring during our fishing trip, we get some Florida Hoppers from Paul and have a shrimp boil. These pink shrimp with a distinctive red spot on their tail are the perfect boiling shrimp.

I make this tasty salad from the leftovers of our shrimp boils. I peel the shrimp and chop them up into bite-size pieces and I cut the corn kernels from the cob. My rule-of-thumb is to use about equal portions shrimp and corn. Toss those two ingredients with a little Tasso ham, jalapeño, cilantro, and olive oil and you have a tasty salad or dip to serve with your favorite chips. Tortilla chips work great; but try sweet potato chips like the ones we make at the restaurant. That's my favorite.

Also, when choosing your olive oil, look for the best extra-virgin olive oil you can find. A vibrant, fresh, and fruity oil will really brighten up the dish.

- ¼ CUP DICED TASSO HAM
- 2 POUNDS FRESH GULF SHRIMP, BOILED WITH CRAB BOIL SEASONING AND CHILLED
- 4 EARS OF CORN, BOILED WITH CRAB BOIL SEASONING AND CHILLED
- 1 FRESH JALAPEÑO, SLICED RAZOR THIN
- ¼ CUP FRESH CILANTRO LEAVES
- 2 TO 4 TABLESPOONS EXTRA-VIRGIN OLIVE OIL
- KOSHER SALT

PLACE THE TASSO into a skillet over high heat and cook until browned, 2 or 3 minutes. Transfer to a paper-towel lined plate to drain and cool to room temperature.

Peel the shrimp and coarsely chop into bite-size pieces. Place in a large mixing bowl.

Remove the kernels from the ears of corn and add to the shrimp.

Add the Tasso, jalapeño, and cilantro to the shrimp and toss to combine. Add just enough olive oil to coat the mixture and give it all a good sheen. Season with salt to taste. Cover and refrigerate until ready to serve.

Cooking Tip: *At the restaurant, we grind red pepper flakes in a coffee grinder to make a dried seasoning that we use like salt. Sprinkling a little over a dish adds flavor and heat, but does not burn like cayenne. It's the perfect finishing touch to just about anything, including this salad.*

SMOKED CHICKEN SALAD

SERVES 6

On a fishing trip years ago down in Venice, Louisiana, I made a batch of this chicken salad. Venice is one of those fishing destinations that you need to bring your own food … or go hungry! I was the cook for the trip and this chicken salad was a huge hit with the group.

In fact over the years, it's kinda become legendary! When I arrive at the dock, the first thing my friends ask is if I brought the chicken salad.

Not only does it taste good … but it's super convenient to eat on the boat. I make a big batch, put it in a plastic container, and throw it in the cooler. I bring a bag of dollar rolls on the side for serving. The guy with the cleanest hands opens up a dollar roll, scoops out some chicken salad, and passes it down the line. Lunch is served!

Cooking Tip: *At the restaurant, we always have vinegar-soaked mustard seeds on hand. We use them to flavor lots of different things … from vinaigrettes to slaws to salads like this one. They add a great flavor to just about anything.*

FOR THE CHICKEN BRINE:
- ¼ CUP KOSHER SALT
- 1 TABLESPOON GRANULATED SUGAR
- 1 TABLESPOON BLACK PEPPERCORNS
- 1 BAY LEAF
- 1 QUART WATER
- 8 CHICKEN THIGHS

TO BRINE THE CHICKEN:
Combine all the brine ingredients, except for the chicken, in a 2-quart sauce pot and bring to a simmer. Cook until the sugar and salt are dissolved. Remove from the heat and chill in the refrigerator to less that 40°F. Once cooled, place the chicken thighs in the brine (making sure completely covered in brine), cover, and place in the refrigerator for 5 to 8 hours.

TO SMOKE THE CHICKEN:
At the same time you brine the chicken, place the mustard seeds and the vinegar in a small bowl and let the seeds soak, for at least 5 to 8 hours or up to overnight.

Prepare a smoker and balance the fire at about 225°F to 250°F. Use cherry wood chips or the wood as directed by the manufacturer of your smoker. Smoke the chicken thighs until the meat falls off the bone, for about 2 to 3 hours. Allow the chicken to cool to the touch and then pick the meat from the bone, being careful to remove any veins and skin. Allow the picked chicken to cool completely in the refrigerator.

FOR THE CHICKEN SALAD:
- 2 TEASPOONS MUSTARD SEEDS
- 1 TEASPOON APPLE CIDER VINEGAR
- 6 OUNCES GOLDEN RAISINS
- 8 OUNCES MISSOURI PECANS
- 2 TABLESPOONS DIJON MUSTARD
- ¾ CUP MAYONNAISE
- ½ MEDIUM YELLOW ONION, SMALL DICE
- 1 CUP SMALL DICED CELERY
- 3 TABLESPOONS CHOPPED FRESH DILL
- 2 TEASPOONS KOSHER SALT

TO PREPARE THE SALAD:
Combine all the ingredients in a mixing bowl. Season with salt to taste. Cover and refrigerate until ready to serve.

SMOKED PENSACOLA MULLET

We make our smoked mullet the night before a fishing trip so that we can enjoy it the next day with ice cold frosties.

It's a tradition that started years ago when I was a teenager. My buddies and I learned how to smoke mullet from Ben Cloud when we worked at The Fish Peddler down on the pier in Gulf Breeze. We all have our own versions of the recipe that Ben taught us and it's always in the cooler when we head out on our annual Cobia fishing trips.

Smoking foods takes time. It is essential that the ingredients being smoked are allowed to soak up and develop the smoky flavor from the wood chips being used. The time it takes to smoke a dish depends on numerous factors such as the size of the pieces, quantity in the smoker, the type of smoker, and even the weather. On average, it takes me about 2 hours to smoke the mullets we catch. That said, it can take as little as an hour, or sometimes up to three hours. The trick is to check the fish to see if it is done. I prefer the fish to be relatively dry and thoroughly cooked.

- 1 MESS OF VERY FRESH, ICE-COLD MULLET
- 50% KOSHER SALT
- 35% GRANULATED SUGAR
- 15% LIGHT BROWN SUGAR

TO PREPARE THE MULLET:
Remove the heads and guts. Split open each mullet along the back and through the rib bones, keeping them still connected at the belly. The backbones can be left on one side or removed. The skin and scales should be left on. This will leave the fish in a slight triangle shape with the tail at one corner and the two top "shoulders" of the fish at the other corners.

Using a paper towel, clean out the black liner of the belly cavity. This is best done without using water if possible as water on fish flesh will soften it quickly and cause the finished product to not be as firm. Plus, when heading mullet, it is often possible to pull the entire entrails and head out in one clean piece. This takes practice, and if necessary, the cavities can be rinsed until you get it down.

TO PREPARE THE DRY RUB:
This recipe is in ratio form so you can make as much (or little) as you need. We eyeball our mix ... but what is most important is that the mix is 50/50 salt to sugar. Of the sugar half, about 1/4 is brown sugar.

Sprinkle an even coat of the dry rub liberally over the flesh and bone side of the mullet, using approximately 1 tablespoon per fish.

Wrap the fish in plastic wrap, place in the refrigerator, and allow the fish to rest and marinade with the rub for 1 hour.

TO SMOKE THE MULLET:
Prepare a smoker and balance the chamber at around 225°F. Use your favorite wood. I prefer to use pecan or sassafras for this recipe; but in a pinch, I will use cherry or white oak.

Place the fish on the racks of the smoker in a single even layer, skin side down. Smoke until a nice color forms and the flesh is cooked through, for about 2 hours.

Remove the fillets and allow to rest at room temperature for 30 minutes to an hour to allow the smoke to "bloom." Then cover with plastic wrap and refrigerate for several hours before enjoying.

ACKNOWLEDGMENTS

JENNIFER CHANDLER: The anatomy of a recipe, even (and sometimes especially) ones written by award-winning chefs, can be presented on the back of a beverage nap or in unfamiliar but delicious code. Jennifer, cookbook author, food stylist, radio host, and restaurateur, savors recipe editing and chatting with chefs. Skilled, precise, with quick-fire results, she caters to every cook. Yum.

LEANNE KLEINMANN: Smoothing transitions, checking consistency, spelling, and style are essential tasks because they matter. And just when you think the narrative is perfect, Leanne sends a redline indicating the most compelling sentence in your copy has no subject, though she does it kindly and with a smile. And she can write alluring copy after a fishing-guide interview. Period.

RANDY P. SCHMIDT: A skilled New Orleans digital and film photographer, Randy preserves memories through a collaborative and adaptive lens. Schedules collide sometimes and our primary photographer had to be out of the country. On short notice, Randy brought his expertise and affable attitude to the waters of Delacroix, LA, and went with the flow. Smile.

DOXA: Of course branding of Susan Schadt Press and design expertise for the publication of my fifth and sixth books would be entrusted to the design dream team of Corrie Blair, Ryan Slone, and principal Tim Walker at DOXA Total Design Strategy, Inc., in Fayetteville, AR. Collegiality, expertise, and innovation are routine and brilliance is not uncommon. A tag line I saw recently on a DOXA client's annual report: "Expect More." Exactly.

CHARLIE MCCRORY (MY DAD): It took a few decades for the DNA to kick in but most weekends, year round, my daughter Canby heads to the water with my dad's refurbished Abu Garcia Ambassador reels and a boat load of exhilaration. Fischer, my grandson in Colorado, is 5 and has been fishing since he was 2 and is fated by fishermen on both sides of his family. He already outcasts many adults. I grew up fishing with both of my parents but mostly my dad. It is one of the greatest gifts he gave our family. He always wanted me to publish a fishing book. Love.

MR. DAISY: To those in the know, my husband Chuck's working title was bestowed upon him by Billy Dunavant several years ago. Yep, for years he has driven me far and wide, patiently listening to my conference calls, copy, and children checking in. I am grateful for his tireless work of enduring the companionship, or lack thereof, of a spirited spouse. Adore.